TRACING YOUR ANCESTORS' LIVES

FAMILY HISTORY FROM PEN & SWORD

TRACING YOUR ANCESTORS' LIVES

A Guide to Social History
for Family Historians

Barbara J. Starmans

Pen & Sword
FAMILY HISTORY

First published in Great Britain in 2017
PEN & SWORD FAMILY HISTORY
an imprint of
Pen & Sword Books Ltd
47 Church Street
Barnsley
South Yorkshire
S70 2AS

ISBN 978 1 47387 971 3

Typeset in Palatino and Optima by CHIC GRAPHICS

Printed and bound in England by
CPI Group (UK), Croydon, CR0 4YY

Pen & Sword Books Ltd incorporates the imprints of Pen & Sword
Archaeology, Atlas, Aviation, Battleground, Discovery, Family History,
History, Maritime, Military, Naval, Politics, Railways, Select, Social History,
Transport, True Crime, Claymore Press, Frontline Books, Leo Cooper,
Praetorian Press, Remember When, Seaforth Publishing and Wharncliffe.

For a complete list of Pen & Sword titles please contact
PEN & SWORD BOOKS LTD
47 Church Street, Barnsley, South Yorkshire, S70 2AS, England
E-mail: enquiries@pen-and-sword.co.uk
Website: www.pen-and-sword.co.uk

CONTENTS

PREFACE

Concentrating on the history of the UK, *Tracing Your Ancestors' Lives* is not intended as a comprehensive study of social history but instead an exploration of the various aspects of the topic of particular interest to you, the family historian. This book is a guide to your journey beyond the names, dates and places in your pedigree charts back to the time and place where your ancestors lived. Use the research advice, resources and case studies in this book as you learn about your ancestors, their families and the society they lived in and record their stories for the generations to come.

ILLUSTRATIONS
All the illustrations are from the author's collection except those for which another source is given.

Chapter 1

INTRODUCTION

WHAT IS SOCIAL HISTORY?

Social history is the study of the lives of ordinary people, a view of history from the bottom up, instead of from the top down. Rather than studying politics and wars or memorizing the successions of kings and queens, learn about the day-to-day lives of your ancestors and place them in the context of their time and place. Journey back through the centuries to experience how your forebears lived, worked and played. Learn about their occupations, their homes and their communities to understand their views on religion, family and traditions. Your ancestors are not just names and dates. They each have a story to tell, a life full of triumphs and tragedy, punctuated at times with hope and at others with despair. They loved, and they lost. They succeeded, and they failed. Like us, they took several steps forward and then were pushed back by circumstances beyond their control. They faced difficult decisions and hard times. They hungered for sustenance, for love and for life in times and places that are at once very different but in other ways so very much the same as the four dimensions of our own world. Our ancestors are the people that we would most like to meet, the ones who shaped our fates and determined our destinies. It is time we got to know them.

SOCIAL HISTORY AND GENEALOGY

The surface area of our planet is about 196.9 million square miles and there have been 525,600 minutes in every one of the years that have passed since our ancestors were born and died. Within that immense time-space continuum, it is estimated that over 107 billion people have walked on earth since man first appeared. Even by limiting our view of social history to just the most recent millennium and to the 94,000 or so square miles of the United Kingdom, the dimensions of all those yesterdays are astounding in their apparent infinitude, and are beyond the scope of this book. Instead, throughout the chapters in this guide to social history, you will learn how to research the circumstances of your own individual ancestor's life so you can tell their story with the objectivity, empathy and compassion that comes from a thorough understanding of the realities of their era.

Imagine that you could draw up a chair by the fire at your ancestors' house and have a cup of tea with them. Don't you long to ask them not just the who, when or where questions, but the more important questions of how and why? If only it were possible to travel back in time, our research would be so much easier. Instead, use the study of social history to view your ancestors' life stories from their unique perspective instead of through your own twenty-first century eyes. As you learn more about their circumstances and the time and place they lived in, you will become more familiar with your ancestors' lives and be able to surmise what forces drove them to the decisions they made and the paths they chose to follow.

As you begin what will be a journey to research your family's social history, you will learn how to determine the demographics of the area that your ancestor called home. Understanding the people and families who lived and worked in their neighbourhood is one way you will get to know your ancestors just a little better. You will also learn about ethnicity and religion and the prejudice these sometimes inspired. You will study the social currents that flowed through your ancestors' time and place and learn about the customs and traditions they cherished. You will research such topics as alcohol consumption, drug use and sexuality which are generally considered a twenty-first century phenomena but that actually date back into the mists of time. The institution of marriage was one of the pillars of your ancestors' lives, an expected rite of passage between childhood and adulthood. You will learn about the social pressures they felt to wed and understand the limited options that were available when a match went wrong. You will research educational opportunities and child labour statistics and uncover what these meant for your ancestors' children that were fortunate enough to survive infancy.

Your ancestor's home, whether it was a sprawling country estate or a cramped one-room tenement, was the cornerstone of their existence. You will study the challenges they faced in a world with little sanitation, no running water and no electricity. You will uncover the unique and sometimes severe environs in which they lived. From the isolated rural villages to the vermin-infested towns and cities to the stately manor house on the hill, their place in time was quite different from our twenty-first century world. Learn about the energy that women had to put into keeping their homes clean and research the challenges involved with completing simple tasks like doing the laundry or making a meal for the family. From bustles and hooped skirts to pantaloons and breeches, our ancestors wore considerably more clothing than we do, but it was certainly not unusual for a common man or woman to own only one or two changes of apparel because of the high cost of a dress or suit.

Uncover the fear and superstition that surrounded mental health issues and learn about the quackery and charlatanism that often passed for medical care in Victorian times. Try to understand what it meant for our ancestors to have children knowing they might lose them before their first birthday to infection or disease they were powerless to prevent or cure. Contemplate a world where an epidemic of disease might wipe out entire households and a time when garlic, vinegar and smoke from the fire might be the only defence against deadly ailments that killed tens of thousands. Imagine wearing your grief for all to see in the form of black apparel, donned according to custom for a year or even a lifetime.

You will learn what it was like to measure income against the price of a loaf of bread, sometimes coming up short of the amount necessary to feed the family and having to go, hat in hand, to the parish for help. Your ancestors might have toiled from well before sunrise until long after sunset for six or even seven days a week, just to exist. Their occupations, learned from their father and from their father's father, might have been made redundant by new technologies and new expectations.

For many of our ancestors, signing a document might have meant simply making their mark and receiving a letter might have meant having to find someone to read it to them and to pen a reply on their behalf. Like us, they probably enjoyed their holiday times and had their customs and traditions. They may have gone eagerly to church each Sunday or have been compelled to attend by social pressure or government decree. Our ancestors may have had to weigh the hunger resulting from not having eaten for days against the penalties of death or transportation if they were caught stealing food from their neighbours.

And with each passing generation came new challenges, new opportunities and new choices. Were the colonies really a place where the roads were paved with gold and the rivers ran with honey or would they be sorry to have left behind what they had, little as it might have been? Should they abandon the ways of the past and embrace the wave of the industrial future or were they right to regard the new ways with suspicion and distrust? Was the speed of the steamships and railways worth the risks or were the old ways of walking and travelling by coach better and safer?

Our ancestors faced these types of challenges, not too different from the trials we face in our own lives. And like each of us, they had to find their own answers, ones they could live with and ones that were right for their own circumstances. According to Ernest Hemingway, 'when people talk, listen completely. Most people never listen.' To understand our ancestors, we need to walk in their shoes, to feel what they felt in light of their experiences and their unique situations. This is a difficult enough challenge with our own nuclear families and our friends but when you add in the complications of never having met our ancestors and never having experienced life in their century or place, it is even more important to listen. Only by really listening to their voices can we hear their stories through the muffle of time.

Each of the following chapters will highlight a general area of study and will offer examples, case studies and a listing of resources for further research. Everyone's ancestors will be different and each will have a unique story to tell and it is up to us, the social historians of the family, to tell their stories in ways that will capture the imaginations of all the generations to come. I hope you will be inspired to research the relevant subjects relating to your own ancestors until you feel as though you know them, celebrating all that is good and fine about them while understanding and forgiving the rest.

RESOURCES

There has never been a better time to be a social historian. Every day, more and more previously obscure books, journals, diaries and newspapers from across the centuries are being digitized and made available to read online, bringing us the tools for understanding life in the time of our ancestors through a basic internet search.

Digitized Books and Journals

There have been many books written about history. On my own shelves, I have a book that claims to tell the history of the world in 618 pages and another that offers 449 pages on just the history of salt. Both are excellent and informative and well worth owning and reading. But the best books for learning about social history are not about history at all. They are the books about everyday life *from* history. That is, the non-fiction books that were written by contemporaries of our ancestors on subjects like cookery, housekeeping, beekeeping, raising sheep or making a quality quill pen. There are many digitizing projects in progress for these older books and more of these one of a kind texts are being put online with searchable text every week. Links to the websites mentioned here can be found in the appendix.

Book scanner at the Internet Archive Headquarters. (Wikimedia Commons)

Google Books is probably one of the best-known resources for digitized books. Use the search tools in the Google Books search to limit your results to only free Google eBooks published in a given century or custom time period. When you find an interesting book, add it to your Google Books library so you can easily find it again later. Millions of books have been scanned since the Google Books project started in 2004 although scanning efforts appear to have slowed in recent years. Many of the historical books are presented in fully searchable text that can be read in a browser or downloaded in PDF or ePUB format. Other, more recent books are available in a limited preview format and although they cannot be read in full, they can be searched and you will find links either to buy the books from a reseller or to locate them in a nearby library.

Google Books search tools.

Internet Archive eBooks.

Another popular resource for digitized books is the Internet Archive, an online non-profit library of free books, journal articles, sheet music, audio, video, old archived websites and more. Their digitized text collection offers over eight million public domain eBooks on a wide range of topics. Create collections of your favourite books and read them in your browser or download in PDF, ePUB and other popular formats.

On the Europeana website, find books, newspapers, letters, diaries and archival papers from many of Europe's leading galleries, libraries, archives and museums including the British Library. Other websites that offer digitized books include the Hathi Trust Digital Library, Project Gutenberg, Open Library and Family Search Books. The British Library website also provides direct access to 68,000 nineteenth-century volumes on subjects including philosophy, history, poetry and literature, and offers links to free websites with digitized books in their 'Help for Researchers at Home' section. For manuscripts, archives and digitized works on the history of medicine, the Wellcome Library is a growing archive, easily searchable by keyword. Look for titles that have been scanned and made available on CD or as a download on Archive CD Books Britain.

jStor is a rich archive of articles from scholarly journals for the arts, sciences, social sciences and humanities available by subscription or through your local library. Find nineteenth-century medical or engineering journals with articles on various topics. Other journals and articles are available from the same resources as digitized books including Google Books and the Internet Archive.

Another excellent online resource for digitized texts is the British History Online website, a non-profit digital library from the Institute of Historical Research through the University of London. Online since 2003, and completely overhauled in 2014, it includes more than 1,250 volumes from many libraries, archives and museums and is fully searchable.

New resources for digitized texts are popping up every day. Find new archives with an internet search for 'digitized books online public domain' or similar keywords.

Print Books

When you are unable to find a digitized version of a book, one of the best places to search for physical books is in World Cat, the website with largest network of library content and services. Give World Cat your location and search for books and other materials on your subject of interest in the library closest to you. Choose to view all editions and formats when searching since the book may have been scanned and made available in eBook format somewhere online. If the book you find is only available in print format and not in a library close to you, many institutions can obtain the book through inter-library loans. Create an account on World Cat and track your favourite books, create lists and save searches. Check eBay for old books in the antiquarian and collectible category or visit a local antiquarian book dealer to find old and out of print books.

Images, Audio and Video

A picture can be worth a thousand words. For a visual bridge back to the past, search for paintings, engravings and drawings of people, places and events from times past or, in more recent periods, search for photographs. From the time that photography was first commercially

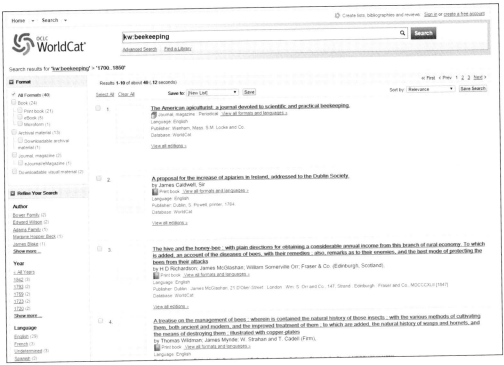

Use World Cat to find library books.

introduced in 1839, millions of photographs have preserved the social history of our ancestors, showing them at work, at home and at play, giving us an insight into their lives that words in a book never could. The invention of the phonograph by Thomas Edison in 1877 gave rise slowly to the preservation of the voices of the past and some early recordings, like images and books, have been digitized. And finally, at the turn of the twentieth century, the film industry provided us with moving pictures so we could see the lives of our ancestors in motion.

Many of the archives that host digitized books also have collections of images, audio materials and video clips from the public domain. Copyright laws differ for various materials depending on when they were created, who created them and whether the creator is still alive so take care to read any copyright notices on materials you find.

Quite possibly the fastest growing archive website, Internet Archive has 2.6 million audio clips and 2.1 million video clips and over 1 million images hosted on their website. Europeana, the digital resource website, also stores images, sounds and video files on their servers. Their images include paintings, drawings, maps, photos and pictures of museum objects while their audio offerings include music and spoken word from cylinders, tapes, discs and radio broadcasts and their video collection comprises films, newsreels and television broadcasts.

The British Library has an online audio archive that includes recordings of arts and literature performances, classical music, environment and nature, popular music, sound recording history, world and traditional music, and oral histories. Another interesting feature of their online audio offering is the accents and dialects recordings that are accessible through an interactive map.

One of the best websites for public domain images, sounds and videos is the Wikimedia Commons website. For more historical video clips, visit YouTube and search on your topic of interest along with keywords like 'history'.

A great tip to find historical images is to perform a search in Google Images and then limit your results to just those in black and white. When you find an appropriate image, don't forget to make sure that the image is not under copyright restrictions and always credit the photographer when using any media in your family history research, even when in the public domain. For a more comprehensive explanation of copyright laws, refer to the UK Copyright Service website or consult a lawyer.

Maps and Gazetteers

Social history is about time and place and there is no better way to visualize a historical time and place than by consulting a historic map. Some of the best maps of the United Kingdom from the eighteenth and nineteenth centuries were developed as a result of events that took place in the time of our ancestors. In the aftermath of the Jacobite rebellion of 1745, it was recognized that the army had no accurate maps of the Scottish Highlands and in 1747 a survey of the Highlands was commissioned to produce a series of maps of the area. This was the beginning of the Ordnance Survey of Great Britain, the maps it produced providing an excellent resource for the social historian.

There are many types of maps, each having its own benefits for social history research. Use topographical maps to see the physical landscape and to find hills and valleys, rivers and coastlines. Newer maps will show man-made features such as roads, canals and railways that might suggest migration and travel routes that your ancestors could have

followed. Boundary maps are primary for showing civil and administrative boundaries or counties, districts or parishes, helpful when trying to
establish where to look for your ancestors' records. Land use maps are
maps that delineate land use such as areas designated for forest and
woodland, arable land including fallow, rotation grass and market
gardens, meadowland and permanent grass, heathland, moorland and
rough pasture and primarily urban areas.

One of the most comprehensive websites for Ordnance Survey maps
is the Old-Maps website. Search your place of interest and locate a map
from the time frame you are researching. Order a digital map in PDF
format or a physical print map or subscribe to the monthly subscription
service to view close-ups of the online maps.

A website with a similar name, Old Maps Online, offers a gateway
to over 400,000 historical maps in libraries around the world. Their
website highlights two significant collections from the map library of
the British Library. One of these is the Ordnance Surveyors' drawings
from the first survey of Britain between 1780 to 1840 and the other is
the Crace Collection of maps of London from 1570 to 1860. Another
noteworthy collection is from the National Library of Scotland which
features over 100,000 maps of Scotland and Great Britain including
some town plans. Another contributor to the website is the University
of Manchester Map Library including its excellent collection of maps of
the north-west of England and the city of Manchester.

The Vision of Britain website also has an extensive map library
including topographical maps, boundary maps and land use maps from
the early twentieth century. Their site uses a seamless map view of
several series of maps including the ordnance maps, assembling the
separate sheets into a single zoomable map of Britain.

Originally produced to aid insurance companies in accessing fire
risks, fire insurance maps for urban areas are incredibly detailed and
include the footprints of buildings, their use (commercial, residential,
etc.), the height, number of floors and the construction of the building,
invaluable for visualizing the neighbourhoods where your urban
ancestors lived and worked. The British Library website has an excellent
collection of fire insurance maps dating from 1886 to 1930.

Used alone, or in conjunction with historic maps, gazetteers offer a
listing of towns, villages and parishes, often with a description of the
area, a brief history and population at the time of printing. They usually

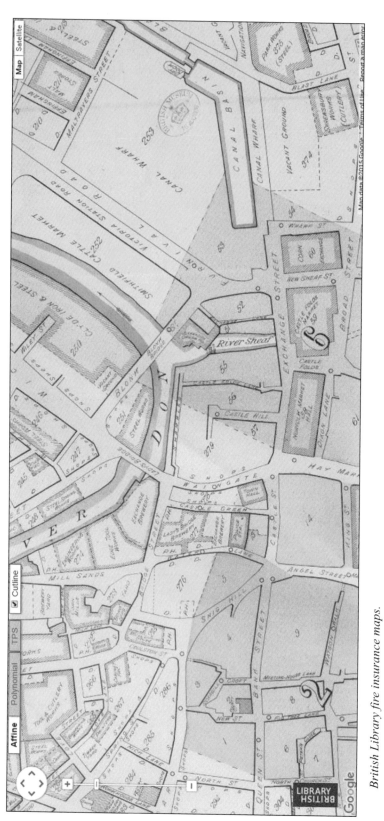

British Library fire insurance maps.

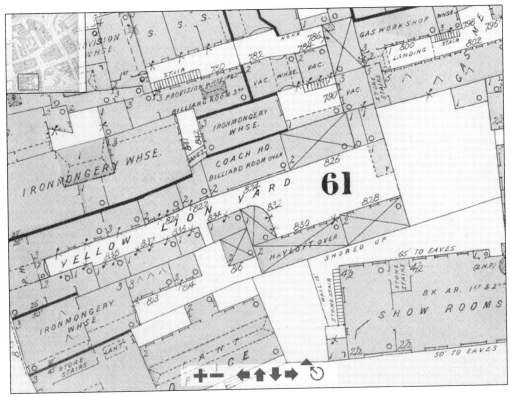

include the distance from nearby places, making them helpful for locating small villages, manor houses and other obscure places on maps. Gazetteers can be found in digitized book archives and for a searchable gazetteer with a wealth of information, visit the Genuki website. Their online gazetteer covers England, Ireland, Wales, Scotland and the Isle of Man. Use it to find places, view online maps and to find genealogical resources associated with a place.

Research Papers, Reports and Statistics

One of the great things about history is that regardless of whether research was done yesterday, during the last few decades or even centuries ago, the information in the resulting papers and reports won't have changed with time. From statistics gathered after the decennial censuses, to studies commissioned by Parliament in the mid-nineteenth century, there are countless historical sources of information about your ancestors' time and place.

The website A Vision of Britain Through Time has compiled data sets from many sources to give historical statistics about population, industry, social structure, learning and language, agriculture, life and death, work and poverty, housing and religion and ethnicity. Explore reports compiled from census data from 1801 through 1971 ranging from simple popula-tion reports to detailed reports on occupations and mortality.

Another source of demographical information from the censuses are the reports that were created shortly after the decennial censuses were taken and many of these reports were published and have been digitized. For example, a report, available through Google Books was published in 1860 on the occupations of the people and the increase in population between 1841 and 1851. In it, many occupations are discussed along with an analysis of where each occupation was most commonly practised. In the Sudbury district, there were 158 people engaged in wig-making, while in Birmingham, there were 470 men and 90 women occupied as toymakers. In St Pancras, there were 180 men who built organs. Statistics add context to your social history research.

Use Google Scholar to find research papers and theses on subjects of interest. Some of the articles found might be hidden behind paywalls but others are freely accessible in PDF format and can contain great information as well as a bibliography of other sources to explore.

In 2013, the Society for One-Place Studies website was founded and since then, many members have initiated studies of places in England, Ireland, Scotland and Wales. A one-place study is about people and families in their geographical and social context in a specific location. Someone might already have researched your place of interest, providing a wealth of detail about it, but if not, you may want to consider registering your own study. It is by learning about your ancestors' neighbourhoods, villages or towns that you will come to understand them better.

Letters and Diaries

Letters and diaries give us a very personal view of history. They allow us to view the time and place through the eyes of the author. Even though your own ancestors might not have left written evidence, it is possible that some of their contemporaries might have done so. Look for letters or diaries of people that had something in common with your ancestors. It might be that they shared an occupation or were involved in the same war. They may have lived in a similar area or shared similar circumstances.

Unfortunately, there is no single repository for letters and diaries, so finding relevant examples can take some creative searching. Try searching with keywords like 'diary online England 1800..1900' or 'letters doctor 1700..1800' and substitute your own area of research. Interest in old letters and diaries is growing and many historians or societies are embarking on projects to scan or transcribe these treasures. Find letters and diaries that are not yet online in the manuscripts and private papers held by private archives, record offices and libraries. Some of these may be hiding amongst the uncatalogued items in their collections while others may be listed in repository finding aids. A search of the National Archives Discovery catalogue for the keyword 'diary' finds over 125,000 entries for record in the National Archives collection and close to 53,000 in other archives around the country. A similar search for 'letters' returns over 1.5 million results.

As one example of what you might hope to find, the Stirling Council Archives has transcribed the Georgian diaries of Dr Thomas Lucas of Stirling, written between 1808 and 1821. These diaries include Dr Lucas' views on Stirling, his family and business life and on both local and international events taking place at the time. Another example is a collection of a sailor's letters written during his voyages between 1754 and 1759. These letters were compiled into a book titled *Sailor's Letters Written to His Select Friends in England During His Voyages*, published in 1767. The volume has been digitized and is available on Google Books.

Newspapers
The Polish poet Stanislaw Jerzy Lec once said that 'the window to the world can be covered by a newspaper.' And even though not everything in the newspapers in our ancestors' time and place was true and certainly some newspapers published articles that reflected the extreme biases of the editors, historical newspapers are still one of the best resources a social historian can use to absorb the atmosphere of their ancestors' world.

Search for news articles about events of national or regional importance or read letters to the editor to gain an insight into contemporary opinion and beliefs. Look for family notices or obituaries to learn more about the lives of your ancestors and the people they knew. Even advertisements, such as classifieds, shipping notices and products for sale, will open a window into the daily life of yesterday. Beyond search, try simply browsing a newspaper title from your time and place of interest to expand your familiarity of your ancestors' world.

The growing newspaper collections of the British Library span more than three centuries and take up over 20 miles of shelving in the purpose-built National Newspaper Building at Boston Spa, West Yorkshire. Researching in these historical newspapers used to mean painstaking manual searches in paper volumes or microfilms but several digitization projects are changing this forever.

As scanning technology became more advanced in the early 2000s, the British Library made plans to begin digitizing some of its vast collection of nineteenth-century titles. The result of that project is that about two million pages from national and regional newspapers spanning the years 1800 to 1900 are accessible free from the British Library. In a similar digitization project, 1,270 titles and well over 900,000 pages from the seventeenth- and eighteenth-century Burney Newspaper Collection are also available through the British Library.

More recently, in a partnership between the British Library and Findmypast, about 40 million newspaper pages are being digitized in a decade-long project already well under way with over 12 million pages scanned at the time of writing. These print pages have been digitized at high resolution using optical character recognition or OCR, making it possible to search articles by name, location, date or keyword. The scanned collection can be accessed through the Library's reading rooms, by subscription on the British Newspaper Archive website from any browser or through a subscription to the Findmypast genealogy website.

Another British historical newspaper resource includes the London, Belfast and Edinburgh Gazettes accessible through The Gazette website where you will find notices of royal honours and awards, military, state, transport and planning notices, notices of corporate or personal insolvency and deceased estates notices. The Gazette was first published in 1665 in Oxford at the time of the great plague.

Other resources not to be overlooked include digitized newspapers from Britain's colonies which often include British news and opinion. The Trove website from the National Library of Australia features Australian newspapers from 1803 to 1954 and is free to all. The Library of Congress Chronicling America website hosts American newspapers from 1846 through 1922 and is also free. Find more online newspaper resources by an internet search with keywords such as 'British newspapers historical online'.

Websites

Since the introduction of the World Wide Web in the 1990s, the number of websites online has grown from a mere 130 sites in 1993 to somewhere around a billion today. If you were to try to visit all the websites in the world, spending only a minute on each one, it would take you over 1,900 years to complete your tour. How then can we find information relevant to our social history studies? The sheer enormity of all the available information seems a little overwhelming.

The most powerful research tool for the internet is a search engine such as Google, Yahoo! or Bing. Read and learn the advanced search techniques for your favourite search engine. Most search engines support using double quotes to find a phrase such as "blind asylums" or "historic pubs". Use a minus sign to omit a search term from your results. Suppose you are searching for an overview of the history of the Isle of Wight in the south of England but your search results are also showing the history of the Isle of Wight in Virginia, United States. Use the minus sign to limit the results: 'history of Isle of Wight –Virginia – VA' will find all results for the history of the Isle of Wight that do not include Virginia or VA in them. One of the more useful search operators for historian is the year range. Use a search term such as 1800..1900 to limit your results to those containing mention of years within this range.

Another way to find your way around the web is to use referrals. A popular directory of genealogy related links, Cyndi's List, began in 1996 with just over a thousand links to websites around the world and has grown to over 333,000 links with more being added every day. Links on Cyndi's List are categorized into various subjects, with categories being further broken down into sub-categories. Many other websites also include helpful referral links. The British Library website is vast and besides the material and collections they offer, they also have links to resources outside the library's site. The National Archives website has an extensive research guide section and many of the guides include not only finding aids for the National Archives collection but links to other helpful websites.

Another tremendous resource for information on virtually any subject is Wikipedia, a free, online open source encyclopaedia. Since the inception of Wikipedia in 2001, it has grown into one of the most often referenced websites as more than 70,000 volunteers contribute to the millions of articles hosted in 290 languages. Opponents of Wikipedia argue that, by the very nature of its model of openly-editable content, it may contain information that is less than reliable, while supporters cite the same reasons why the information found there is, for the most part, accurate. Regardless of which camp you might fall into, Wikipedia is a great place to start researching any subject of interest in your social history journey. Use the information found as an overview and then follow the citations and references found at the bottom of each article to locate other resources on the same subject.

In the past, finding out what was on offer at an archive or record office often meant accessing the card catalogue on site, flipping through index cards to find records of interest. Most archives now offer at least a part of their catalogue online and some catalogues even contain links to content that can be accessed online. For example, use the National Archives Discovery catalogue to search not only the resources at the National Archives but also at more than 2500 archives across the UK. Millions of records are available for immediate download for a small fee.

Since our primary goal is to view history through the eyes of our ancestors and their contemporaries, websites that offer first-hand accounts of events are excellent fodder. One of these is the Eyewitness to History website, maintained by Ibis Communications, Inc, a digital publisher of educational programming. This website provides articles about various events in history by referencing eyewitness accounts from books, letters and diaries. Although somewhat American-centric, it nonetheless has articles from Great Britain's history such as an account of a London hanging in 1726, William Harrison's views on crime and punishment in Elizabethan England and the coronation of Queen Victoria in 1837 as recorded in her diary.

When you find a particularly relevant website for your research, find others like it with a Google search using the related operator. As an example, searching 'related:eyewitnesstohistory.com' will return a list of similar websites such as History Net, a World History Group website that includes over 5,000 articles previously published in their magazines.

Timelines

Put your ancestors' lives in context by learning what was happening in their location, their country or the world during their lifetime. There are countless examples of historical timelines online that can be used as reference. Some are general in nature and others are specific to countries or particular subjects. The BBC History website offers an interactive general timeline from 854 BC through to the present day. The British Library website also has an interactive timeline that explores English history through the evolution of the English language and examples from literature such as an illustration from a news book published in 1607 and *Robert Cawdrey's Table Alphabeticall*, the first English dictionary published in 1613.

More specialized timelines include the Victorian Web timeline of the Industrial Revolution or the BBC History timeline of the Civil War and Glorious Revolution spanning the years from 1603 to 1714. There are timelines for just about every subject of social history research from the history of railways to the medical discoveries of the Victorian age. Search for 'timeline <subject>' to find examples and assemble a timeline for your ancestors' lives.

Genealogy Websites and Databases

The Family Search website has millions of historical records that are free to search. Other popular genealogy websites such as Ancestry and Findmypast are subscription-based although they can sometimes be free to access from local libraries and family history centres. Make an effort to search out the records about your ancestors which offer social history clues. Wills and letters of administration often give insight into your ancestors' lifestyles. Land and tax records can give hints about their homes. Parish chest records such as vestry minutes, poor records, settlement records, apprenticeship records and church warden accounts might offer invaluable nuggets of information about family situations or leads to interesting stories.

Beside their obvious use for searching for records related to your ancestors, consider using genealogy databases for your social history research as well. Explore census records in your area of interest to get an idea of the demographics of the neighbourhood. Compare the same neighbourhood decade after decade in the census to see changes in the community. Browse a city directory by street to understand whether an area was residential, commercial, industrial or a mixture of the three. Leaf through parish registers of baptism, marriage and burial records to get an understanding of the congregation. What were the common occupations? What were the average ages of the brides and grooms?

What was the average age at death? Do you notice any clusters of burials that might signify a local epidemic of a disease?

In Ancestry, enter only a date or place and a keyword and search their extensive databases to find records of possible friends, neighbours and associates of your ancestor who share a particular characteristic. For example, in the census records, search for your ancestor's birthdate, their town of residence and enter their occupation in the keyword box to find possible work colleagues. Browse the genealogy website card catalogues for digitized books, maps, newspapers, periodicals or other useful databases that may not appear in ordinary search results.

SHARING YOUR FAMILY'S SOCIAL HISTORY

As genealogists, we all want to share our research with our families, but most non-genealogist's eyes simply glaze over when they are presented with pedigree charts and family group records. That is where social history comes to the rescue. Even the most history-averse family members will love a good story with a plot full of conflicts and struggles. Paint a picture of your ancestors' world with your words and any images you've been able to locate related to their time and place. Don't recite a series of names and dates. Show, don't tell, their story. Use the context of their neighbourhood, their friends and acquaintances, their occupations and their homes to add detail and interest to your narrative.

Stories based on real events are often referred to as 'creative non-fiction', a genre of writing that uses the styles and elements of fiction, poetry or memoir to recount actual events. It sometimes blurs the lines between fact and fiction but is grounded by the historical evidence from your genealogical research. Whether you write an account of your ancestors' lives in a book, share it in blog posts, get creative with scrapbooks or create a multimedia presentation online, it is the story that matters. Regardless of length or medium, a good story has the same elements: a setting, some characters and a plot with a beginning, a middle and an end.

Setting

Get to know your setting by researching your ancestor's time and place. You should be able to take your reader to the place you are writing about, conjuring up an image in their mind with sights, sounds and smells from the past. What was the weather like on the day that your great-grandparents were married? What were the conditions in textile factories during the time period that your ancestor worked in one? If the family home is still standing, find a description of the interior or if it has been demolished, then describe a similar home. View a map of the area from the appropriate time period and learn what the locale looked like. What route would your ancestor have travelled when they went to work or to the shops? What events were taking place locally during the period of your story?

Characters

Above all, get to know your ancestors intimately. If possible, learn what they looked like by finding photographs, drawings or physical descriptions of them. At the very least, learn what their contemporaries looked like and describe what you do know about them. For example, if your ancestor worked as a butcher, you might describe their stained canvas apron, the slightly coppery metallic smell of the blood and the tools of their trade.

Plot

Choose portions of your ancestor's lives to include in your story. The best plots begin with a conflict or a struggle, whether with another character, with life situations or an internal struggle. The story goes through twists and turns, with the tension getting higher towards the end of the story and finishes with a triumph (or sometimes a defeat).

Styles or Types of Creative Non-fiction

Creative non-fiction can take many forms. You might write a personal essay or memoir about your own life or ancestors that you knew. You may choose to write about your ancestors' lives from further back, of whom you have no personal knowledge. One of the most difficult decisions when writing creative non-fiction is finding the right blend of creativity to weave into the historical research process. As genealogists, we've been trained to stick to the facts, while at the same time, we want to tell a compelling story to capture the reader's interest and it is our social history research that will give us the authoritative voice when adding the descriptions and imagery that will bring our stories to life.

Chapter 2

PEOPLE, FAMILY AND SOCIETY

As genealogists, our fundamental focus in our social history research will be the people, families and the societies in which they lived. Our ancestors and their friends and acquaintances will be the characters in our stories, animating historical facts and breathing life into the events of the past. If you were a journalist writing an investigative article about someone, you would interview them to learn their point of view and to capture the essence of who they were. Unfortunately, we aren't able to schedule an afternoon to sit down with our ancestors and ask them questions about themselves, but we can still use our social history research skills to learn about them, the surrounding people, the customs they observed and the traditions they maintained.

Just as the different communities we visit in our own time have a certain rhythm and cadence, so too did the places that our ancestors lived. We can research the society they were part of, uncover the social currents that flowed through their lives and listen to the voices of our ancestors' time and place. By equipping ourselves with the knowledge of their place in society, we can better understand their choices and the paths they followed.

The progression of our ancestors' lives probably followed the same pattern as the lives of their parents and the same as the lives of their neighbours and friends. There were less choices available to them. The constraints imposed upon their behaviours were perhaps more stringent but at the same time, these constraints made their lives far less complicated than life in our time.

Our ancestors' families were most likely founded on the institution of marriage. Men and women were expected to marry after they reached a certain age and they were expected to stay married, through good times and bad, in sickness and health, as long as they both should live. Children usually were born soon after marriage and every couple of years afterwards and families were often large. In most families, the children had only a few years to play or attend school and then were sent out to work at an early age, contributing their salaries to the family income. As parents grew older and could no longer work to support themselves, they went to live with their married children who cared for them until death. Life for our ancestors was, in most cases, a predictable arc.

In earlier times when travel was both difficult and expensive, our ancestors were more likely to have stayed close to home and their local community was the centre of their world. Whether they were part of the elite upper class, or were the poorest of the lower class or somewhere in between, our ancestors socialized with those around them, those that shared their economic circumstances, their standard of living and those who believed in the same values and ideals. The people who lived around them were their friends, their neighbours or sometimes perhaps even their enemies. By learning about those people, we can better envision the lives and times of our ancestors.

Although it's likely that most our ancestors spent the majority of their time working, they would have looked forward to whatever leisure time they could manage. Those in service might only have had one day off each month and an evening to themselves each fortnight. Factory workers in the early nineteenth century might have worked twelve-hour days throughout the week with a shorter, nine-hour day on Saturday, with only Sundays free. Farmers, of course, worked every day during the busiest seasons of ploughing, planting and harvesting but took their free time during the winter months when there was little to be done except maintenance and repairs.

Whatever their situation, our ancestors would have made the most of their free time whether they visited with family, stepped out to the local pub, or planned a day's entertainment at a fair or other attraction. If our ancestors were of the more privileged classes, their leisure hours would have been more plentiful and their choices for entertainment would have been more varied. They might have attended the races at Ascot or visited friends at their country estates for a weekend of hunting.

Regardless of how your ancestors spent their time off, learning more about the activities they chose to take part in will bring you to a better understanding of the type of person they were. If they joined an association such as the Foresters, they believed in helping others in need. If they played an instrument with the local band, then perhaps they were a musician at heart. If they entered produce into the local fair, it is possible they had pride in their farming roots.

And if your ancestors did spend their free evenings in the local pub indulging in a pint or two, they were certainly not alone. From the early eighteenth century, duty records show England consumed over 3.1 million barrels of strong beer and almost 2 million barrels of small beer each year, with combined annual totals topping 6 million barrels by the turn of the nineteenth century. Beer was not the only popular alcoholic beverage either. By the middle of the eighteenth century, at the height of what has been called the 'Gin Craze', the British were consuming 2.2 gallons of gin per person each year. While habitual drunkenness might generally have been considered a habit most associated with the lower classes, alcohol abuse could be a problem for people from any station. It was not until the nineteenth century and the dawning of the industrial age when the medical community began to realize that excessive consumption of alcohol might be due to addiction and not just related to a weakness of character. Some of our ancestors may have indulged a little more than they should while others may have been involved in the temperance movement, eschewing alcohol in any form.

At the conclusion of this chapter, after you have researched some of the subjects relating to your ancestors' personal lives, their families and the surrounding society, imagine you really were able to sit down for an afternoon and interview those who came before you. How many of your questions would you already know the answers to? What more can you learn and how many more questions have you thought of asking them?

DEMOGRAPHICS

Every neighbourhood, every town and every county has its own particular demographic, that is a series of statistical data relating to the population and particular groups within it. Modern estate agents help prospective buyers to pre-qualify properties for sale by describing the demographics of the immediate area so a purchaser can decide if they and their neighbours would be a good fit. Most people tend to live near other people who are very like themselves. A neighbourhood is likely to be made up of people who are from the same social class, the same level of economic prosperity and who share a similar ethnic and religious background.

Consider your own neighbourhood and the neighbourhoods you have lived in over your lifetime. What could a newcomer learn about you and your family by learning about the other people and families that live in your neighbourhood? Take a mental walk around your community, look at the houses and visit the local shops and businesses. Watch the people as they go about their gardening and lawn care and the children as they play in the yard. Now take a step back in time and try the same exercise in your ancestors' neighbourhoods.

Back when our ancestors were alive, the enumerators for the decennial censuses did just that, walking their assigned streets and calling at each household and recording details of each family. Between 1801 and 1851, the population density of England had grown. Whereas in 1801 when the first census was taken, there was, on average, one person for every 153 yards, by 1851, there was one person for every 108 yards. Put another way, someone visiting 100 houses in 1801 would have to travel 20.6 miles, but in 1851, the same person would need to travel only 14.3 miles.

By using the demographical data collected in the time of our ancestors, we can learn about their friends and neighbours and in so doing, we can learn more about our ancestors themselves. The decennial census data from the nineteenth century is an invaluable resource but even before 1800, there are some data sets that we can turn to for insights into our ancestors' communities. Parish registers and historic tax records are useful although sometimes imperfect resource and we need to exercise care we don't draw the wrong conclusions when our available resources are incomplete.

Our ancestors' community would have changed over their lifetime, just as the populace in localities of our time can metamorphose. Some changes to the demographics of a place come from the ebbs and flows of births and deaths, a process known as natural transformation. Other demographical changes are due to people moving to a locality or away from it, a process known as internal migration. By studying the makeup of our ancestors' communities over time and looking at occupations, ages and family units, we can make inferences based on the population change about possible causes such as mortality and fertility of the people, immigration and emigration, employment opportunities and the economic vigour of the neighbourhood.

Case Study – Pig Street, Kingswinford

The Black Country is an area of the West Midlands just north-west of Birmingham. It was so named because of the black soot that covered the area during the industrial revolution as coal and coke mines, iron foundries and other industries were established in the area. The Turner family moved to Kingswinford, Staffordshire in 1850 and remained for two decades. This case study uses maps, detailed census data, census statistics and reports from the mining commission.

It was about 1850 when the Turner family moved from Pensnett to Kingswinford, a distance of only two miles along the Dudley road. At 39 years old, Emmanuel Turner was one of the older miners living on Pig Street. His Irish wife Winifred was also 39 years old and their daughters were Elizabeth, aged 8; Jemima, aged 7; Martha, aged 5; Margaret aged 2 and Eliza at just 7 months. Their only son, Benjamin, was 5 years old.

A geological fault-line effectively divided the parish of Kingswinford in half, with one half being agricultural land and the other half rich in coal and ironstone. With the chief seam of coal about ten yards thick and near the surface, more than 3,000 acres of the parish were covered in collieries. By 1851, with the industrial revolution driving demand, almost a million people in Great Britain were working in minerals and metals of various kinds, with over a quarter of those employed on coal, either mining it from the earth, distributing it to consumers or manufacturing it into coke and gas.

Pig Street (now Hartland Street) ran east-west, just south of High Street between Machin Street (now Bell Street) and Church Street and was home to thirty-five families. Over two-thirds of the men were in their twenties or thirties and all but two worked in the mines, mostly as coal miners but a few as ironstone miners. Over 80 per cent of the Pig Street residents were born in the Black Country counties of Shropshire, Staffordshire and Worcestershire and most of the rest came from the industrial counties of the north. Mining had been a going concern in the Pensnett area since the latter part of the eighteenth century with the opening of the Stourbridge Canal in 1779, but it was most likely the opening of the Kingswinford line of the Oxford, Worcester and Wolverhampton railway in 1847 that resulted in new mines being developed and drew the Pig Street miners to the town of Kingswinford. By 1851, internal migration within England was rising with many people moving to counties where mining and manufacturing operations were active. Indeed, Staffordshire's population had increased due to immigration from other counties by almost 40,000 people.

From 1842, when the Mines and Collieries Act was passed by the Parliament, boys under 10 years old and all women and girls were prohibited from working underground in coal mines. In 1851, Winifred Turner, like the rest of the wives living on Pig Street, was at

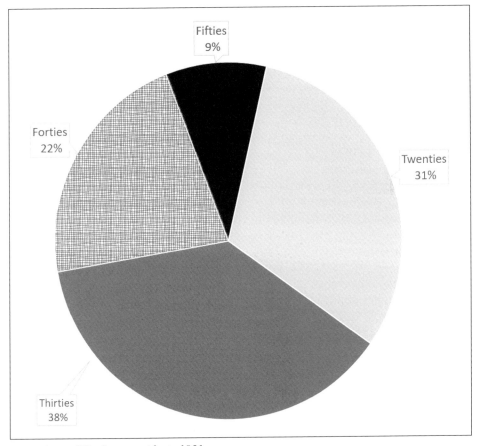

Ages of Pig Street residents 1851.

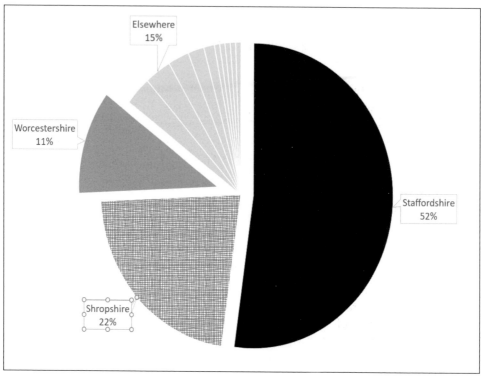

Birthplaces of Pig Street residents.

home looking after the children. Although about a third of the children on the street attended school, the Turner children did not. The Turner's only son Benjamin was just five, but it was likely, like the rest of the Pig Street boys, by the age of 10 or 11, he would go to work in the mines with his father.

Indeed, by 1861, the Turners' son Benjamin, aged 14, was a labourer in the mines alongside his father who worked as a sinker. The younger children: Margaret aged 12, Eliza aged 10 and James aged 8 were attending school, an opportunity the older children never had. The population of the parish had grown about 20 per cent in the earlier decade from 27,301 people in 1851 to 34,257 people in 1861 and coal mining was still the prevalent industry. The occupations on Pig Street had become more specialized, and the men were now pudlers, blast furnace men, watchmen, sinkers, engine fitters, forge men as well as coal miners. Winifred, with her older children now working out or married and her younger children now in school, took in laundry to supplement the family income.

By 1871, the Turner family had grown, and the children had moved elsewhere. Emanuel had gone to Rowley Regis to work as a sinker while Winifred stayed behind on Hollies Street in Kingswinford, with only their 20-year-old daughter Eliza left at home. Unlike many miners of his time who died quite young, Emanuel lived to the age of 66, when he succumbed to heart disease in 1877. Winifred survived him by five years, dying in 1883 of cardiac disease and asthma in the home of her oldest daughter.

Resources

From 1801 to 1831, the census in England, Wales and Scotland was collected by parish rather than by household. While individual records rarely survive, statistics relating to these censuses can be found on the website A Vision of Britain Through Time and more detailed tables can be found in books published by the government after the census data was collated. Many of the census publications have been digitized and are available on digital book websites such as Google Books and Internet Archive.

The census taken in 1841 is notable because it was both the first household and the first nominal census, recording each person, including their name, approximate age, occupation and birthplace whether in the same county as the return, or in Scotland, Ireland or 'foreign parts'. From 1851 through to 1911, the census remained much the same, although more detailed questions were added. Statistical information was gathered from these enumerations as well and can be found in the same places as those for the 1801 through 1831 censuses. Histpop is another online resource of published population reports created by the Registrars-General for England, Wales, Scotland and Ireland for the period 1801–1920, as well as census reports for the period 1801–1937.

As genealogists, we are familiar with finding our own families in the census records but there is a wealth of information to be found about our ancestors' friends and acquaintances in the census pages before and after. Today, there are many resources for census images, both paid and free, and most of these offer an opportunity to browse the record sets.

Begin by locating a census record for your ancestor and then browse to the beginning of the forms to find the front page. This front page will usually contain the name of the enumerator along with a detailed description of the enumeration district and sometimes even a hand-drawn map or notes from the enumerator. Use this description to locate the neighbourhood on a map contemporary to the time. Browse the record from the first page all the way through to the last. Create your own demographical statistics for your ancestor's neighbours and friends. How large were the families? How old were the people? Were they born locally or did they come from other counties? What were their occupations? Did the children attend school? How many rooms did the average house contain? Collate your results and compare and contrast your ancestors to their contemporaries to form a picture of your ancestor's family in relation to the families in their neighbourhood.

Before civil registration began in July 1837, and even afterwards, the milestones of birth or baptism, marriage and death or burial were recorded in parish registers. From 1538 when records were first mandated, the level of detail is diverse, but even from the more common rudimentary entries, some demographic data can be extracted. Infant mortality can be measured by finding baptism entries followed by burial entries. Family sizes can be extrapolated from baptism records. Life span can be determined by comparing baptisms with burials. While most early registers have sparse detail, a few contain fascinating details including birth order of children, or ages and even causes of death.

ETHNICITY, IMMIGRATION AND SOCIAL CURRENTS
The British Isles have a long history of invasion and immigration. The earliest known immigrants to Britain were the Celts and the Picts who settled before written history and formed some of the first communities. The Romans first invaded in 55 BC and they were followed by the Angles, the Saxons and the Jutes who arrived in increasing numbers after the Romans left in about the fifth century. The Vikings came too, with the earliest Viking invasion being in the late eighth century. Then in 1066 the Duke of Normandy, William the Conqueror, invaded Britain and is perhaps best remembered for his great survey of England in 1086, and the resulting Doomsday Book.

The second millennia saw the arrival of the French Protestant Huguenots from about 1670 as they fled religious persecution in France and came to Britain in numbers estimated to be between 40,000 and

50,000 people. They settled primarily around London and many became involved in textile manufacturing, with large silk workshops being established in Spitalfields.

At about the same time, several smaller groups of immigrants came to Britain. Italian exiles came in the early nineteenth century after the Napoleonic Wars destroyed agriculture in Northern Italy. Indians arrived in England aboard the vessels of the East India Company, sometimes remaining behind when the ship sailed, becoming servants to the gentry.

Africans too, transported on the transatlantic slave ships that called into Liverpool before the 1807 abolition of the slave trade, would escape from their ships and often become servants or nursemaids to upper-class families. Other Africans came from the British colonies with their slaveowners when the children were sent back to England for their education. By 1770, there were about 14,000 black people resident in England and in 1772, the legal case of Somerset v Stewart was heard and in a judgement at the King's Bench, slavery was found to be unsupported in Common Law. The black population of England was effectively emancipated by the ruling, although slavery would not be abolished throughout the Empire until the Slavery Abolition Act was passed in 1833.

The next large group of immigrants to arrive in England were the Irish, who came primarily between 1830 and 1850, fleeing the poverty of Ireland in the wake of the Potato Famine. Impoverished and desperate, the Irish were not welcomed. They were willing to accept very low wages, effectively taking jobs from the English working class. Many sent their wages earned during the summer months back home to Ireland to pay rent there and relieve the poverty of their families left behind. By the winter, with no savings left, they became dependent on parochial relief in England, with removal to their home parishes in Ireland being prohibitively expensive, for although passage from Dublin to Liverpool could be had for a shilling, return passages were being charged at four times that amount.

Germanic immigrants arrived in England throughout the centuries, journeying across the North Sea. They numbered over 37,000 in England by 1881, with occupations ranging from servants and bakers to teachers and merchants and although most made their homes in London, they were well represented in the industrial towns of

Liverpool, Manchester, Cardiff, Leeds and Birmingham. Prince Albert, husband of Queen Victoria, was of the House of Saxe-Coburg and Gotha, a German dynasty that was renamed the House of Windsor in 1917 because of anti-German sentiment during the First World War.

Despite these steady influxes, Britain's population remained relatively homogeneous throughout the eighteenth and nineteenth and well into the twentieth century, although foreign-born residents did number almost half a million people by 1900. It was not until the Aliens Act of 1905 that Britain even had any immigration controls to speak of, with the Home Secretary assuming responsibility for immigration and nationality matters.

The stated purpose of the 1905 Act was to keep the poor and criminal elements out of the country, but in practice, it targeted the large numbers of Eastern European Jews who came to England after 1880, fleeing religious persecution. Tens of thousands of poor and unskilled Jewish immigrants settled in the East End of London in the three decades between 1880 and 1910 and as a result, rising anti-Semitism triggered the formation of the British Brothers League who exploited immigration fears.

How did your ancestors feel about the various groups of immigrants that came to Britain throughout the centuries? Were they curious about the cultural differences or did they resent the drain the newcomers placed on the economic resources of their parish, their county and their country?

Case Study – The Stockport Riots of June 1852

The riots in Stockport in June of 1852 made international news. This case study examines the underlying tensions and the prejudices towards the Irish Catholic community that sparked the confrontation in Stockport and follows the inquest into the tragic death of Michael Moran, a 23-year-old Irishman through contemporary newspaper accounts.

On Tuesday, 15 June 1852, just weeks before a general election, Lord Derby's Tory government issued a proclamation to prevent and repress processions of Catholics wearing the habits of their orders and exercising the rites and ceremonies of the Roman Catholic religion on highways and places of public resort. The prohibition had been law since the passage of the 1829 Roman Catholic Relief Act, and many saw the proclamation as a political ploy to garner support from the anti-Catholics. Despite this proclamation, the Irish Catholics of Stockport were led on such a procession by their priest on Sunday, 27 June and tensions began to build.

The following day, Monday, 28 June, William Walker, a 30-year-old shoemaker, entered the Bishop Blaise public-house with his mate John Charlesworth at about 7 o'clock in the evening. A scuffle over a hat ensued and the innkeeper, William Hough, asked the two men to leave and after some resistance, they went out into the street. Shortly afterwards, a group of about six Irishmen came in with their wives and daughters to enjoy some ale and some dancing. About 8 o'clock, the innkeeper heard a shriek in the taproom and entered to find that the Irish were thrashing Walker, who had returned. He was again asked to leave and eventually was led out of the house. About a half hour later, Walker was seen in the street opposite the end of Barlow-row. Two Irishmen came up Hillgate and Walker followed them and struck one on the head. He kicked at the other but missed and one of the Irish picked up a stone and threatened to throw it before they retreated back down Hillgate. Walker met up with about thirty men at the bottom of Edward Street and about the same number of Irishmen stood at the end of John Street, about 300 yards away. The two groups converged and a punch was thrown. A fight ensued but the disturbances subsided when the police arrived.

On Tuesday afternoon, a gang of factory lads armed with sticks began running up and down the streets. An Irishman was attacked by the mob and by evening the crowd numbered 500 or 600, with some carrying axes and swords. The mob began throwing stones, breaking windows and slashing at railings of the Irish houses and fighting broke out in the streets.

It was about a quarter before ten when the military arrived and as the mayor read the Riot Act to those assembled, a new report was received of property being destroyed in Edgeley. Some of the forces were diverted to the scene in Chapel Street and there they found a fire burning in front of the priest's house, fuelled by his furniture, chapel fittings, books and papers. The windows of the nearby chapel and the schools were smashed and all the doors had been demolished. Even the interior of St. Michael's Chapel had been destroyed by the mob.

One man, Michael Moran, was killed in the course of the riot. The jury brought in a verdict of 'wilful murder' against Michael Mulligan, the young man charged with the assault. Moran, also an Irishman, had become engaged in a scuffle with an Englishman by the name of Wood. Wood was hit with a stone and he grabbed Moran and they both went down. An Irishman, presumably aiming for Wood, struck Moran on the left side of the head. As Wood worked himself free, Mulligan ran up, also striking Moran on the left side of the head. That blow resulted in Moran's death a few hours later. That Mulligan had also been aiming for the Englishman Wood seemed unlikely since at the time of the fatal blow, Wood had pulled away from the fracas. More likely, with tempers flaring in the confusion of the brawl in the street, the blow had been struck without consideration of Moran's nationality.

The 18-year-old Mulligan was committed for trial at the Chester Assizes but after less than an hour of deliberation, the jury returned a verdict of manslaughter rather than murder and Mulligan was sentenced to fifteen years' transportation.

A magistrate's inquiry was convened to investigate the details of the Stockport riot. Despite the hundreds that had taken part in the riot, only twenty prisoners were committed for trial. With passions still running high amongst the English and Irish of Stockport, the magistrates were perhaps keen to make sure the indictments would not be judged unfair by either side and in the end, of the twenty bound over for trial, ten were English and ten were Irish.

Mulligan, who had killed one of his own countryman in the melee that night, was one of the Irish prisoners. Among the English was William Walker, who had initiated the drunken brawl with the Irish in the Bishop Blaise public-house that Monday evening. That Walker targeted the group because they were Irish, or whether he was simply drunk and spoiling for a fight, did not come up during the trial, but it is almost certain his young wife Rose Ann, herself a native of Ireland, was not impressed with her husband's behaviour.

During the trial, all the Irish but only three of the English were found guilty.

Resources

While historical newspapers are certainly among the best resources to gauge popular opinion, care must be taken to read accounts from many sources, to obtain a full understanding of the affairs of the day and to avoid the sometimes partisan viewpoint of any particular newspaper.

In the case study about the Stockport riots, while all the newspapers in July 1852 agreed the disturbance in Stockport was both serious and disgraceful, they did not all agree on the root cause. Many blamed Derby's government for the entire affair, claiming the proclamation of 15 June incited the riot. Some papers, including the *Daily News*, held the Catholic Irish responsible for starting the riot saying 'The Irish population have been unhoused, the Saxons having taken fearful retaliation upon the Irish Catholics, who commenced the riot breaking the windows in St. Peter's Protestant School.' Other newspapers, including the *Morning Chronicle*, blamed the English, noting, 'After the sack of the "Irish quarter" of that town [Stockport], the Government will doubtless rest satisfied that they will find plenty of "supporters" to rally round them in defence of our "Protestant institutions".' Very detailed accounts of the riot appeared in international papers as well, but the tone of these arm's-length articles was somewhat less partisan.

Magazines, periodicals and pamphlets are also a tremendous resource to measure the prevalent attitudes of the British population. Known internationally for its satirical cartoons, the first edition of the magazine *Punch* was published on 17 July 1841 and by the turn of the century, circulation had topped 50,000. No longer in publication, *Punch* offers an online gallery of over 18,000 images from the nineteenth and twentieth centuries spanning the years from 1841 through 1992. Look for other historical magazines, periodicals and pamphlets on digitized book archives and search for them online on specialized websites like *Punch* and on archive, library and academic websites.

For detailed insights into Jewish immigrants who settled in the East End of London in the late nineteenth century, explore the four notebooks of the Charles Booth Online Archive relating to the community. One notebook has letters, booklets and interviews about the Jewish population in 1897 while three other notebooks focus on the textile trades of tailors, bootmakers and hatters. Another great online resource relating to the history of the Jewish community in Britain is the Virtual Jewish World which offers an overview of Jewish history in the United Kingdom from 1066 to the present day, as well as providing brief histories of the communities in many urban cities such as Birmingham, London, Liverpool, Nottingham and Warwick.

Records relating to non-British citizens who arrived in England between 1810 and 1869 can also be found on Ancestry. These records come from record sets held at the National Archives and were created as a result of various acts passed in Parliament which were the earliest attempts at monitoring or regulating immigration into the United Kingdom.

The standard genealogical resources can also be searched for statistical information and overall knowledge about Britain's immigrant population. Census records from 1851 to 1911 include a specific place of birth, a searchable field in most online databases. If your ancestors were immigrants, search for other people with the same birth place to find out where they were living. Was your ancestor part of a community of his or her compatriots or did they settle in a more homogenous area of the country?

CUSTOMS AND TRADITIONS

A few years ago, I bought my grandchildren the latest Christmas craze, the Elf on the Shelf. That saucy little elf character looks much like my own elf that hung in the dining-room window, monitoring my every move when I was a child. But stories of elves and fairies observing and guarding human children are far older than I am and stretch back into the folklore of our ancestors. In fact, many of the customs and traditions we enjoy with our families today were passed down through the generations from our ancestors of long ago. The holly that drapes our mantelpieces harkens back to the days of the Druids and the eggs we decorate at Easter are reminiscent of the elaborate eggs that were ornamented with gilt and given as gifts in centuries past.

Some traditions, such as dancing around the maypole to celebrate May Day, have enjoyed a resurgence in our time after being neglected for centuries. An ancient ritual, maypole dancing had become increasingly popular in the latter part of the Middle Ages, but after the Reformation in the sixteenth century, maypole dancing was viewed as a heathen practice that led to wickedness and many of the village maypoles were destroyed or re-purposed. It was only toward the end

THE ELVES' SUPPER.

'The Elves' Supper' from St. Nicholas: A Monthly Magazine for Boys and Girls (1875–6). (Public domain)

of the nineteenth century that some villages brought back their maypoles and the traditions surrounding them.

Other customs, like the traditional pranking of April Fool's Day, have never gone out of favour and no doubt our ancestors took part in the foolery from time to time. In a 1795 newspaper article, one man wrote of his grandfather who as a boy would stalk through the churchyard at night, wrapped in a tablecloth, hide the maid's shoes, blacken his face to frighten the children or grease the strings of the chaplain's violin, proving boys will be boys, no matter the century.

New Year's Day, which we celebrate on the first day of January, used to be celebrated by our ancestors on 25 March as the Feast of the Annunciation before the adoption of the Gregorian calendar in 1752. *Auld Lang Syne*, one of the songs we still sing today on New Year's Eve, was written by the poet Robert Burns in about 1788 and was probably a favourite of our great-great ancestors too. Other New Year traditions of the past included cleaning the house, taking the ashes from the fire and clearing all debts before the church bells sounded at midnight. The custom of 'First Footing' is still common across Scotland, with tradition dictating that the first foot in the house after midnight should be a dark male and that he should bring gifts of coal, shortbread, salt, a black bun and, of course, a dram of whisky. And as in our time, our ancestors would have made New Year's resolutions, and probably broke them.

Three weeks before Easter, mid-Lent Sunday was known as Mothering Sunday, the day for visiting parents and relatives, and a day when adults returned to the towns and villages in which they grew up. It was customary for those in service to be given a holiday on this day and when the census taken on 30 March 1851 coincided with Mothering Sunday, many servants were absent from their employer's houses and some dwellings were recorded as uninhabited.

Samuel Pepys wrote in his diary of Valentine's Day and mentions several people who asked him or his wife to be their Valentine, but in 1668, Pepys decided they should be each other's valentines every year: 'I rose and my wife, and were merry a little, I staying to talk, and did give her a guinny in gold for her Valentine's gift' and then added that 'by agreement to be so to her every year; and this year I find it is likely to cost £4 or £5 in a ring for her'. By the mid-nineteenth century, after the advent of the Penny Post in 1840, the custom of sending Valentine

*Greeting card
c. 1915.*

letters became affordable and not less than 422,000 letters were delivered through the post for Valentine's Day 1847.

While we normally think of tradition and custom in relation to holidays and specific times of year, our ancestors observed traditions when marking milestones in their daily lives. Prior to the late nineteenth century, midwives attended women in childbirth, a custom that is making a comeback in our time. On the other hand, our traditions of a white weddings only date back to Victorian times, after Queen Victoria chose a white gown for her wedding to Prince Albert. The custom of wearing black for mourning dates back into the mists of time but the rules and traditions around mourning dress grew very formal in the Victorian era have since relaxed considerably and in our own time, black has become more of a fashion statement than a sign of grieving.

Although specific dishes may differ by region, nothing says tradition quite like food. From Sunday lunches of roast beef and Yorkshire

Dining room decorated for Christmas. (Photograph by Jaime Garcia, used with permission)

pudding to Burn's Night haggis to Ireland's colcannon made of young cabbage and potatoes to Welsh rarebit, certain foods call out to the years of traditions passed down to us from our parents, our grandparents and all of our ancestors before them. Special foods speak of special times. Where our great-grandmothers used ingredients like suet, we look for modern alternatives and where our ancestors boiled stews over an open fire, we use a microwave, but like the generations that came before us, this is just putting our own stamp on the traditions of the past before we hand them down to our own children.

Research the customs and traditions of your ancestors to find the links leading back to the present time. By learning about the things that mattered most in the past you can build a bridge to the present and find the threads that bind your family across time and space.

Case Study – Decorating the Church for Christmas

Decorating the parish church for the holidays generally fell to the sexton, perhaps with help from the ladies of the congregation, and involved making adornments out of the greenery of the season. This case study examines the advice in an essay on the decoration of churches from the mid-nineteenth century written by the Rev. Edward L. Cutts for the Clerical Journal *in 1859.*

Since the time of the Druids, mistletoe and evergreens have been used to decorate for solstice-time celebrations, adding the lively touch of greenery highlighted with the bright red berries of holly to homes across the Kingdom. That same greenery is suited to wrapping the pillars of the church for Christmas, advises the Reverend Cutts, all except for the mistletoe. Why mistletoe should not appear in the church is not fully known, but Cutts suggests asking any sexton of the Victorian era and he will tell you it is so. For it is the mistletoe that was the mystic symbol of the Druids' mid-winter festivities and so perhaps rejected by the first Christian ministers and then the prohibition passed down through the generations that followed.

'Let the holly be the most prominent of your decorations,' says Cutts, 'for it is the prince of evergreens.' Strip off the berries and use them strung in bunches for the best effect. Ivy should be used sparingly, perhaps to relieve a background of yew. Use small twigs of yew and myrtle and box to make small wreathes and to cover frameworks. He warns that using flowers to decorate the church may be unacceptable to its more conservative parishioners, who are generally afraid of any departure from the traditional greenery.

The pillars of the church beg for adornment and should be wrapped with garlands of greenery. The garlands are formed of a rope of evergreen sprigs, with twigs of evergreen tied in bunches along the length of the rope or from a length of twine with the twigs wired to its length, ensuring the foliage is all turned in the same direction.

Arches should be decorated with a trail of green, preferably fixed to splines which can be put up without nails, using a wedge of wood to hold them in place. The plain bare spaces of the walls should be filled with wreathes or crosses of evergreen or with texts spelling out verses most suited to the season. The texts could be made from letters of cloth of one colour stitched to a background cloth of another colour or a more economical method involves drawing letters on strong white paper and then surrounding them with a frame of evergreens. Do not neglect the pulpit, desk and font but decorate them as well, using wire or wood forms covered with greenery. Flags and banners of velvet may be used as further adornment throughout the church.

If there is a lych-gate or other entrance to the churchyard, decorate it festively with evergreen or build an arch of splines to serve as the entrance. If there is a churchyard cross, it should be adorned with a wreath of holly at the intersection of its limbs.

As a final word of advice, Cutts suggested inviting as many of the congregation to help as is possible, to make sure all are most satisfied with the decorations and to inspire a communion between the church members of various classes that could be more easily gained in an evening of shared industry than in a year of parties and suppers. Try to imagine the decorations in your ancestors' parish church and let the images invoke the scent of evergreen across time.

Resources

Our own family traditions can offer the best window to the customs and traditions of our ancestors. Do you still tuck an orange into the toe of a Christmas stocking? Are there specific foods your family enjoys on particular holidays or at family celebrations? So often, these traditions were passed to our parents from their parents and from their parents before them and even after many years, some vestige of the traditions will remain. Talk to older family members about the customs they remember from their own childhood or those their parents may have talked about. There is a joy in shared experiences across the years and it might be time to revive an old custom of long ago before it becomes lost in the mists of time.

The rise and fall of customs and traditions can be found in newspaper articles relevant to your ancestors' era. At times, great controversies were waged in the press over traditional gatherings turned ugly with drink and violence and at other times, the virtues of holiday festivities were extolled in detail down to the foods that were served

A holiday feast.

and the activities that were enjoyed. Celebrations of one year were compared to those of years past, giving us greater understanding of not only our grandparents, but of their grandparents before them.

Look for instructional books on home decoration from prior centuries or for children's stories from long ago. Find historical accounts of holidays, customs and traditions that compare the festivals of our ancestors' forebears to those of their own time. Diaries and letters might mention family customs and traditions the writers had in common with our ancestors. Did your great-grandfather ask your great-grandmother to be his valentine? Did your great-great-aunt receive the gift of a dyed egg bearing her name and the date on some long ago Easter day? Is that the black armband of mourning your ancestor is wearing in that dusty Daguerreotype photograph?

ALCOHOL AND DRUGS

While some might think drug addiction is a new twenty-first century problem, nothing could be further from the truth. In our ancestors' time, narcotic drugs were dispensed by chemists, and were virtually uncontrolled. In 1840, an Essex newspaper reported 'There is not another county where narcotics are so much used as in that of Lincoln' and that 'every second customer who enters the shop of the druggist is it purchaser of opium, laudanum, Godfrey's mixture, or ether'. Just a year earlier, Dr J. Johnson of the Westminster Medical Society told the members 'opium-eating had increased in this country to such an extent as to have become nearly equal in its proportion with teetotalism'.

In *Household Management*, the best-selling book by Mrs Isabella Beeton first published in 1861, opium in various forms was listed as a medication that should be kept in any well-stocked medicine cabinet. Although Mrs Beeton warned that the opium preparations Syrup of Poppies and Godfrey's Cordial should not be given to children unless under the direction of a surgeon, she did recommend doses of opium for constipation due to lead poisoning, fever caused by burns and as part of a remedy for whooping-cough.

According to a Registrar General's report, in 1857, thirty-four people died from opium, two from morphine and a further eighty-nine from laudanum poisoning. Such drugs could be sold by chandlers, grocers, oilman, drapers or any small shopkeeper. Attempts were made to introduce a bill into Parliament to restrict the sale of both opium and laudanum, but it was not until 1868 that such a bill was finally passed. However, after much argument and debate, opium and all preparations of poppies were subject only to labelling restrictions and the 1868 Act specifically excluded patent medicines, many opium-based. Despite the limitations, the new law did have an immediate effect and deaths from opium between 1868 and 1869 declined by almost 30 per cent. It was not until 1908 that opium and all preparations containing more than 1 per cent morphine were finally further restricted, kept under lock and key and only dispensed with a prescription.

Narcotic drugs were only a part of the addiction problem. Alcohol was ubiquitous. Adults drank beer instead of water in almost all instances, with even workhouse inmates being granted rations of the beverage daily. Children were raised on small beer, a fermented beverage that, although it contained less alcohol than strong beer, was still drunk so freely that intoxication could easily result. To most of the population, beer was considered a healthy drink because it was made from hops. In 1722, an astonishing 33 million bushels of malt for the brewing of beer were produced, equating to 36 gallons of beer for every man, woman and child. Beer was considered so healthful, that according to Dr Christian Augustus Struve in his 1802 book on carrying for children, mother's should guard their children from the evils of coffee, and instead give them small beer for breakfast.

Although beer was the beverage of the people, other alcoholic drinks were also commonly imbibed and sometime overindulged in by our ancestors. For most of the seventeenth century, distillation of spirits had been limited to the Distiller's Company and other royal patentees but in 1690, as a result of embargoes against the French, a general permission to distil spirits made from corn or barley was given and the consumption of spirits began to rise. The gin shops cut into the business of the brewers of London and Westminster and they petitioned the government to 'suppress those Nurseries of Debauchery the Gin-Shops'. In response to the growing number of gin shops, an excise licence of £20 and duties of two shillings per gallon were levied in 1729 but still consumption continued to grow. The Gin Act of 1736 more than doubled the cost of a licence and the duty rose to a staggering £1 per gallon. At first, the public rioted in protest, but then they ignored the law and refused to comply. Finally, in 1743, the licence fees and duties were lowered.

By 1751, there were reported to be 17,000 gin shops in the City of London alone and in an effort to bring control, an Act of Parliament mandated licences were required for all taverns and public houses which retailed spirits. Any distillers found retailing spirits in quantities less than two gallons were fined £10. While this new Act resulted in initial reductions in the number of gin shops, they continued to flourish throughout the nineteenth century. In a *Punch* cartoon from 1879, a lost child is shown with a policeman. The ragged little girl was unable to tell the policeman where she lived, who her father was or where she went to school. The policeman whispered to the child 'Where does your Mother get her Gin, My Dear?' and the mystery was solved.

Did some of your ancestors sometimes seek remedies containing narcotics for minor ailments? Did they enjoy their beer or gin a little too much or a little too often? More than likely, as people of their time and place, they did, at least as measured against our more modern standards. We need to view the people and events from centuries ago in the context of their era and in the perspective of their world. One of my own ancestors died in 1874 from excessive consumption of alcohol. Viewed from the twenty-first century, her cause of death might seem shocking but in her time and place, drinking often and to excess was quite commonplace. When viewed through the empathetic lens of a social historian, the only usual aspect of this ancestor's death was that it was actually attributed to excessive alcohol consumption by the coroner who would have more commonly phrased the cause of the death in a gentler way to spare the family.

Case Study – Teetotallers

In the nineteenth century, there were those who thought drunkenness was like the plague; that it influenced men and women in all ranks and stations to live a life of ruin and one bereft of virtue. These were the Teetotallers and their leader was Joseph Livesey. Some thought there was truth in the teetotaller beliefs while others thought the pendulum had swung too far. This case study is based on the biography of Joseph Livesey edited by Weston James (which was in turn based on Livesey's autobiography) along with newspaper accounts of the Teetotallers.

The temperance movement began in Preston, Lancashire in 1832 with members pledging to moderate or abstain from hard spirits. As the movement strengthened and spread, a few members eschewed alcohol altogether promising: 'We agree to abstain from all liquors of an intoxicating quality whether ale, porter, wine or ardent spirits, except as medicine.' Those who took this hard line on alcohol were sometimes referred to as Teetotallers and some went even further, pledging to abstain from all use of tobacco 'either for smoking, chewing, or snuffing, being an idle, vulgar, and extravagant habit, in most instances injurious to health'. One teetotaller, a cow keeper of Chester, even refused to feed his cows on grain from the brewery.

At the head of the temperance movement was Joseph Livesey. Livesey had long been a believer in the temperance movement but early in 1831, he made a vow never to take any type of intoxicants

---

again. Livesey, a very successful cheesemonger, met with fellow tradesmen on the day before his vow. During the meeting, a bottle of drink was passed around and Livesey took a glass. On his way home that evening however, he felt very queer and unwell and on rising the following morning, he made his decision.

A religious man, Livesey once wrote 'I never see anything wrong, but I am determined to see it right,' and in keeping with his beliefs on the evils of alcohol, on 1 September 1832, he drafted the first teetotal pledge and signed it, along with six others. Livesey went on to dedicate his life to the fight for total abstinence, and all the while, he espoused free trade and fought for the humane treatment for the poor, speaking out against the New Poor Laws of 1834.

The Teetotallers, although more extreme, remained part of the Temperance movement in Preston and their pledge of total abstinence was read aloud alongside the partial pledge until 1835 when it was accepted by all members. The followers of the Preston movement were for the most part working men, and about half of them were former drunkards. Over time, a few slipped back into their old ways but most, like Livesey, held to the vow until death.

This accomplishment is made all the more noteworthy when we consider the role drink played in society during Livesey's lifetime. Drink, in particular ale, was considered one of the necessities of life and people from all walks and classes both indulged and

George Brown's British Temperance Pledge.

47

overindulged. Livesey remembers his childhood church where both the gravedigger and his father were drunkards and the bell ringers and church singers were all hard drinkers as was the parish clerk.

In his final thoughts in his autobiography, Livesey admitted that although they had made much progress, they had not had the complete victory he had hoped in his lifetime. He was confident though, that as more men and women chose to abstain from drink, legislation against it would follow and victory over spirits would one day come.

Resources

While typical genealogical records such as death certificates may occasionally afford insight into our ancestors' possible drug and alcohol use, they will only highlight exceptional cases. To gain a more complete understanding of the topic, contemporary resources such as historical newspapers, books written during the period, statistical information and scholarly articles written on the subject will be your best resources.

When searching historical newspapers, be sure to use the vernacular of the day. People in our ancestors' time drank in bars, pubs, taverns, inns and gin shops. They went to chemists, apothecaries and druggists to buy medications. People who took opium regularly were not users or addicts but more likely to be described as 'opium fiends'. When searching in earlier newspapers, remember the old 's' is often interpreted by scanning technology as an 'f'. When searching, try replacing 's' with 'f' to find the maximum search results. For example, as well as searching for 'fiends', also search for 'fiendf'.

Historical books in the seventeenth and early eighteenth century are not likely to contain mentions of alcoholism since it was not a known term until the mid-eighteenth century, when it was introduced by Swedish physician Magus Huss. Likewise, alcoholic only meant something pertained to alcohol. The word was not used to describe someone addicted to alcohol until the late nineteenth century, not surprising since although alcohol consumption dates back centuries, alcohol addiction was really only universally recognized at the beginning of the twentieth century.

From the sixteenth century, the government sought to control, and of course tax, the distribution of alcohol and many Acts of Parliament were passed throughout the centuries. With each successive Act came much debate that can be an excellent resource to help us understand the push and pulls of public opinion on the official laws. Opium and similar drugs became popular as medications in England when Thomas Sydenham introduced Sydenham's Laudanum as a remedy for many ailments in the late seventeenth century. From the beginning of the nineteenth century, many discussions took place between the medical establishment and the government as controls over drugs were sought.

Google Scholar is another great place to search for statistical information and scholarly articles on the subjects of alcohol and drug use amongst our ancestors. As topics of general interest in our society, these subjects have been well researched by historians and graduate students and a wealth of information can be found with diligent searching.

SEXUALITY, MORALITY, MARRIAGE AND DIVORCE

Like alcohol and drugs, we might imagine the topic of pre-marital sex is more suited to a study of recent history, but most of us will find at least a few female ancestors who gave birth to a child less than nine months after their marriage date and perhaps a few birth records which list the father as unknown. What was different centuries ago were the choices available to a young pregnant girl. Most single women, finding themselves with child, married quickly but when that wasn't a choice, they sought other alternatives.

One choice, abortion, practised since ancient times, was made illegal in England in 1803 and punished harshly. Besides surgically-induced abortions, some desperate girls would try medicinal remedies to their situation including concoctions of tansy, penny royal and savin. Commercial medicines such as Beecham's Pills could be purchased at the chemist and were marketed as a laxative from 1849 but were advertised in thinly-disguised terms leaving no doubt as to their intended use.

Illegitimate births declined in England from almost 7 per cent in 1851 to 5.6 per cent in 1871 while at the same time, the age at marriage went down. In this period, England, unlike Scotland, did not recognize legitimacy if a child's parents married after their birth so our ancestors were encouraged to 'do the right thing' and marry quickly to save their child the stigma of being born illegitimate.

WORTH A GUINEA A BOX.

BEECHAM'S PILLS

Are admitted by thousands to be worth above a GUINEA a BOX, for bilious and nervous disorders, such as wind and pain in the stomach, sick headache, giddiness, fulness and swelling after meals, dizziness and drowsiness, cold chills flushings of heat, loss of appetite, shortness of breath costiveness, scurvy, and blotches on the skin, disturbed sleep, frightful dreams, and all nervous and trembling sensations, &c-, &c.

For Females of all ages these Pills are invaluable, and bring about all that is required. No female should be without them. There is no medicine to be found to equal Beecham's Pills for removing any obstructions or irregularity of the system. If taken according to the directions given with each box, they will soon restore females of all ages to sound and robust health.

For a weak stomach, impaired digestion, and all disorders of the Liver, they act like "MAGIC," and a few doses will be found to work wonders upon the most important organs in the human machine. They strengthen the whole muscular system, restore the long lost complexion, bring back the keen edge of appetite, and arouse into action, with the ROSE-BUD of health, the whole physical energy of the human frame.—These are "FACTS" admitted by thousands, embracing all classes of society, and one of the best guarantees to the Nervous and Debilitated is Beecham's Pills have the largest sale of any Patent Medicine in the world.

Full directions are given with each box. Sold by all Patent Medicine Dealers in the kingdom.

'There is no medicine to be found to equal Beecham's Pills for removing any obstructions or irregularity of the system.' Sheffield Independent, *Monday, 22 September 1873.*

Less hidden in our ancestors' period was prostitution, an occupation as old as time. While prostitution itself was not illegal, attempts to limit it can be found in legislation such as the Disorderly Houses Act of 1751 which banned brothels or the Town Police Clauses Act of 1847 which made it illegal for prostitutes to congregate in public places. Prostitution, for most women, was an occupation of circumstance. Women, unable to support themselves, might turn to prostitution as a last resort and more than a few would give their occupation as dressmaker or seamstress to the census taker to hide their true source of income for the sake of appearances. Up until the Victorian period, prostitution was seemingly tolerated by society as inevitable for men of all social classes and a way of life for women in poor economic circumstances. But by the mid-nineteenth century, a less tolerant public sought to end the evils of prostitution and to save cities such as London from moral decay.

But for most of our ancestors, sexuality was private and unspoken and it was meant to be preceded by the institution of marriage. Chances are, most of your ancestors married in the Church of England after banns were called for three successive weeks, announcing their intention to marry in both the bride's and groom's parish churches. The alternative to calling banns was to apply for a marriage licence, something that was normally done mainly by the upper classes since there was a fee involved, or in cases where the bride and groom were in a hurry to get married.

From 1753, when the Clandestine Marriage Act was passed, the state became involved in marriage, mandating couples had to get married in a church or chapel by a minister for the marriage to be valid. Only Jews and Quakers were allowed to marry other than under the Church of England. It wasn't until the Marriage Act of 1836 when non-religious civil marriages were allowed in register offices. This same act also made it legal for Nonconformist or Catholic couples to be married in their own place of worship rather than in a Church of England parish church.

Most marriages would have taken place when the bride and groom were in their mid-twenties and generally resulted in a regular progression of children, one born every two years or so, as long as the

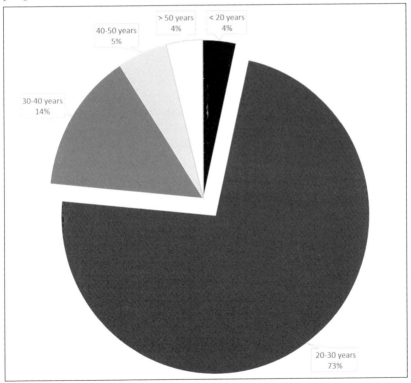

Age at marriage – men.

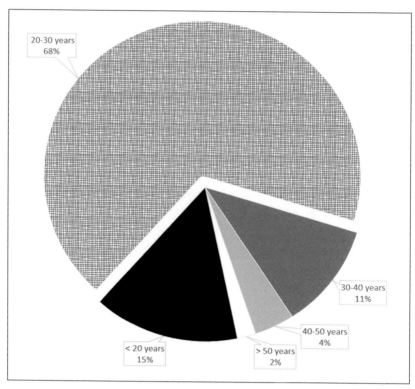

Age at marriage – women.

wife was in her childbearing years. Marriage in the time of our ancestors was, for the most part, 'until death us do part' and lasted until the death of the husband or wife. Life expectancies being what they were, however, it is also likely some of your ancestors would have remarried at least once after the death of a spouse left them widowed, with even third and fourth marriages being common.

Whether or not the husband and wife were happy together, it was the rare case where a marriage would end in divorce. Divorce was not only scandalous, but an expensive proposition, and before the Matrimonial Causes Act of 1858, it required a private Act of Parliament, making divorce available only to the most desperate of the wealthy upper classes. From 1858, divorce was a civil matter and was more accessible. Still, from 1867 to 1886, there were only 5,594 decrees granted for dissolution of marriages while at the same time, there were almost 3.9 million marriages, a divorce rate of just slightly more than 0.1 per cent. Some couples solved the problem of an unhappy marriage by living apart and more than a few men went off to sea, emigrated to another country or enlisted in the Army or Navy as single men to escape their wives. Other unhappy husbands and wives chose to ignore their earlier marriage and risk being charged as a bigamist by marrying a second time. From 1857 to 1904, there were over 5,000 trials for bigamy in England and Wales, but it is likely that there were many more bigamous marriages that were never brought to trial. Others simply lived common-law, with the woman assuming the man's surname, giving the appearance of being married.

Did your ancestors follow the path prescribed by society and marry in their mid-twenties, their children born at two-year intervals? Or is there another story, just under the surface of the records waiting to be discovered? Was a baby born early? Was there an illegitimate child in the shadows? View your ancestors with empathy, for they were a product of their generation in a time where the pressures of society were far stricter than in our time, and where their friends, family and neighbours likely judged them harshly for any transgressions.

Case Study – Baby Farmers

In April 1870, Janet Cowen found herself in the family way. In search of a solution, her father answered a newspaper advertisement from a couple who wanted to adopt a baby, not realizing what evil he had set in motion. The woman he met was Margaret Waters, the notorious Baby Farmer of Brixton. In October, after a sensational trial at the Old Bailey, she would be hanged for the murder of the Cowen baby and others. This case study uses historical newspaper accounts and court records.

Robert Cowen, a musician, lived in Lambeth with his two daughters, Janet and Anne Marie, renting rooms from Mrs Caroline De La Guerra in Loughborough road. When his 16-year-old daughter Janet became pregnant, he made arrangements for her to be confined at Mrs Castle's on Camberwell Road and finding an advertisement in *Lloyd's Newspaper* in May of 1870 from a couple seeking to adopt a child, he wrote to the address provided.

Adoption. —A respectable couple desire the entire charge of a child to bring up as their own. They are in a position to offer every comfort. Premium required, 4l. Letter only. Mrs Willis, P.O., Southampton Street, Camberwell.

On the day following, Mrs Willis responded to Robert's letter, telling him she and her husband who was a shipbuilder had been married for many years but did not have any children and they wanted to adopt a baby. She offered to meet at Brixton Railway Station to discuss the matter further. When they met, Robert explained Janet's circumstances, saying the baby was due in mid-May and they agreed he would write once the child was born to make arrangements.

On Saturday, 14 May 1870, Janet Cowen gave birth to a healthy baby boy and registered his birth, naming him John Walter Cowen. That Monday her father wrote to Mrs Willis, requesting she called at his residence on Tuesday. It was arranged she would take the child that very night. At 9.30 that evening, Robert, accompanied by his landlady Mrs Guerra brought the baby to Walworth Road Station and after a time, Mrs Willis arrived. She admired the baby and wrapping it in a large shawl, she took him and promised to be in touch in a few days.

On the following Friday, Mrs Willis visited the Chaucer road home and said she and her husband were delighted with their new baby and she was busy making clothes for the boy. Remembering the advertisement mentioned a premium, Cowen gave her £2 to cover the expenses of the wardrobe and she left, saying she would call again, but she never did.

Unknown to the Cowens, Sergeant Ralph of the W division had seen Janet Tassie Cowen leaving the midwife Mrs Barton's home on 28 May by four-wheeled cab and followed them home. When he made inquiries, he found she had been recently delivered of a son and it had been put up for adoption with a Mrs Willis through a newspaper advertisement. The Sergeant then searched the newspaper and finding a similar advertisement, he replied to it, saying he had a baby to be adopted. A meeting was arranged and afterwards Ralph traced the woman who had given her name as Mrs Oliver, to a home on Frederick Terrace.

When Ralph called at the house, he asked to see the Cowen baby and was shown a very ill child that was filthy and wrapped in dirty clothes and when he tried to rouse the baby, he could not. He asked

Willis what food or medicine the baby had taken and she replied arrowroot, brandy, milk and sugar, along with medicine ordered by the doctor. She denied having given the child a sleeping draught although a bottle containing laudanum was found on the table in the room.

When the house was searched, ten more children were found, most of them infants. He immediately called Dr Puckle, the medical officer of the district, who examined the children and took them into care at the Lambeth Workhouse. Margaret Waters, the woman who had given her name as Mrs Willis to Robert Cowen and then as Mrs Oliver to Sergeant Ralph, was arrested for failure to provide for the children in her care.

A wet nurse was found for the Cowen infant and although at first it improved, it died of convulsions on 24 June. At a post-mortem on the infant, Puckle found death had been brought on by 'extreme wasting of the body and congestion of the brain' and it was his opinion that the cause of the brain congestion was likely the administration of the narcotic laudanum.

At the trial that followed, Waters admitted under oath that she had for years been looking after illegitimate children for a fee. It was believed Waters had no intention of keeping the infants placed in her care but planned to get rid of them as soon as possible, having received only a few pounds for their care. The house in Brixton was searched and skeletons of babies were found in cupboards, under beds, and even up chimneys.

Margaret Waters was found guilty of manslaughter and executed on Tuesday, 11 October 1870 at Horsemonger-lane Gaol.

On 14 August 1874, Janet Tassie Cowen married John Coward at St. Jude Parish in East Brixton and they went on to raise a family.

Resources

From July 1837 onwards, all marriages were registered at the General Register Office allowing statistical data to be collected for the first time. The abstracts of marriage reports issued by the Registrar General are available on the Histpop website. There you can trace the ratios between marriage by licence against marriage by banns and see the marriages which took place outside of the Church of England growing over time from 1837 to 1920. Prior to 1837, marriages were only recorded in parish registers in your ancestors' local Anglican church. Over time, these registers have been abstracted, transcribed, microfilmed or digitized and can be found in local archives, county archives, libraries and family history centres.

There are, of course, no specific records relating to morality or sexuality in the time of our ancestors, although inferences may be drawn from statistics such as those showing numbers of illegitimate births and often account books of the churchwardens, constables and overseers of the poor, and the minute books of the vestry of the parish may give an insight into the character and circumstances of those who received aid. Paternity for illegitimate children may be difficult to find, although it is sometimes made clear in associated records that show payments made by the reported father for maintenance, apprenticeship and other costs of raising a child.

In old newspapers and other printed materials, references to sexuality will be few and veiled in the language of the time. Reporters might refer to immorality, unnatural activities or indecency without actually naming what they are writing about. In addition to newspapers, criminal records, even those not specifically related to your ancestor, might reveal the undercurrents of society in a time and place.

Divorce, before the Matrimonial Causes Act of 1857, was under the jurisdiction of the Church and required a private Act of Parliament and as such, the proceedings can be accessed through the National Archives website on the Legislation website. From 1858 onwards, divorce became a civil matter and more accessible. Files of the papers related to petitions for divorce can be found at the National Archives and records from 1858 to 1914 have been digitized and are searchable on Ancestry. In either case, newspapers of the time might contain details of the proceedings and the circumstances surrounding them, especially for the more newsworthy cases.

CHILDREN AND CHILDHOOD

In our ancestors' time, the period of childhood was comparatively short. Children from more affluent families were raised by a nanny, hidden away in a nursery until they attained school age, when boys would be sent away to public schools and girls would have been educated at home in the skills of embroidery, music and dance. In contrast, the offspring of the lower classes were sent out to work at an early age, and education was a luxury most could not afford. Poor children worked in coal mines, in mills and factories or as chimney sweeps. Some were put into service, living and working in the homes of the upper classes, and others worked as agricultural labourers. By as early as the sixteenth century, the apprenticeship system provided a means for children to learn a trade. Children, mostly boys but some girls, were indentured for a period, usually seven years, where they worked for, and often lived with, a master of a trade, at the end of which they would be released and be considered a journeyman in that trade. In the seventeenth

Machine used in textile manufacturing.

century, the overseers of the poor were given the authority to place the children of vagrants and paupers into apprenticeships, freeing the parish from paying for their care, and the system expanded.

As the Industrial Revolution got under way in the mid-eighteenth century, families began an internal migration from rural villages to the growing industrial cities and the need for cheap labour grew. Young children, some less than 10 years old, were put to work in the rising number of mines, factories and textile mills. Children not only earned lower wages than adults, they were easier to discipline. By 1821, just less than half of the workforce of England was under the age of 20.

From the beginning of the nineteenth century, however, there was a growing awareness of the perils facing young working children and laws were enacted to protect them from the abuses of the factory system and other industrial occupations. Subsequent inquiries into child labour culminated in a series of protective acts, the most important of which was the 1833 Factories Act. Under the 1833 Act, employment of children under the age of 9 was banned outright while children from 9 to 13 were restricted to working a maximum of 42 hours and children from 13 to 16 years of age were limited to a 69-hour working week. Between 1835 and 1838, the number of children under the age of 13 employed in factories fell from 56,000 to 33,000 and throughout the rest of the century, the laws were expanded to include other industries, workshops and types of factories.

But beyond these laws enacted to protect child labourers, other factors combined to reduce the child labour pool. Technological improvements in textile mills and mines eventually eliminated the menial jobs children had been performing. At the same time, the rising income of families reduced the need for poor parents to send their children to work at an early age and eventually the Compulsory Education Act of 1880 ensured children between the ages of 5 and 10 years of age were in school rather than being part of the labour force.

Even after the passage of the child labour laws and the establishment of compulsory education, poor children lived a very different life than those with more affluent parents. While wealthy children might have meat and cheese daily, the poor would have survived on bread, tea and vegetables with the occasional treat of some dripping. Hunger was not uncommon, and nor were overcrowded and unsanitary living situations with several children sometimes being forced to share a bed, often lying head to toe and toe to head, if indeed they had a bed at all.

Very poor children who resorted to stealing to survive were often caught, arrested and sentenced in the same criminal justice system as adults. Even those as young as 10 or 11 might have a rap sheet listing their earlier offences. Punishment might include whipping, incarceration or in extreme cases, even transportation to the penal colonies. In 1823, when 8-year-old Patrick Ryan stole a fowl from the window of a poulterer, the arresting officer advised the judge that the boy's mother was destitute and he had been led astray by bad companions and the boy was let go with a shilling fine. But by 1840, the courts, overrun with cases of destitute young thieves, began taking a harder line against child offenders. When Thomas Newman, aged 10, was convicted of being a pickpocket for stealing twenty-six shillings, he was ordered to be transported for ten years.

In an effort to provide education for the poor children of London, Ragged Schools were established in 1844, in the hopes an education might serve to lift the children out of poverty. In an impassioned argument to Parliament, Lord Ashley urged the government to consider sending the poorest and most destitute children from the Ragged Schools of London to the colonies, so they might avoid a life of crime. In response, in 1849, the Ragged School Movement received a grant of £3,000 to send 150 children to New South Wales. The following year, Parliament made it legal for Poor Law Guardians to fund the emigration of children to the colonies. These early child migration endeavours gave rise to the Home Children migration schemes of the late nineteenth century that saw more than 100,000 children sent from the United Kingdom to new homes in Australia, Canada, New Zealand and South Africa.

Certainly, by the dawn of the twentieth century, the life of poor and working-class children in England had forever changed with the legislation that had slowly evolved over the course of the earlier century to protect and educate them. As you journey back in time, tracing the generations of your ancestors' lives, consider the opportunities available to the children for education or for employment and imagine their childhoods as they must have been.

Case Study – Child Labour Reform

Joseph Hebergam started working at Bradley Mill near Huddersfield as a young boy and, as a result of his labours there, he became crippled and required an iron brace just to stand. At the request of Richard Oastler, who was fighting for legislation to restrict the working hours of women and children in the mills to 10 hours a day, he bravely testified before the committee at the House of Commons in 1833. This case study primarily references historical newspapers, and traditional genealogical resources.

Joseph Hebergam was just 7 years old when he went to work at George Addison's Bradley Mill near Huddersfield in Yorkshire in 1820, joining his brother John and his sister Charlotte. He worked in the worsted spinning department and attended the throstle machines. His workday began at five in the morning after a mile-long walk from his home. He was allowed a thirty-minute lunch break at noon, although he was required to clean the spindles during that time and he ate his lunch wherever he could, often on the boiler house thatch. His day finished at eight o'clock at night.

There were about fifty other children who worked in the mill, and many of them were often sick. The children were supervised by three overlookers, one of whom was in charge, another who greased the machines, and a third whose sole job it was to wield the strap when the children were not working to his satisfaction. After six months or so, Joseph's knees and ankles began to weaken from the constant stress, causing him great pain and fatigue and in the mornings, he could barely walk. His brother and sister would support him from each side, essentially dragging him the mile from their home to the mill. Sometimes they were late to work and the overlooker would wail them with a strap until they were black and blue. Other times they would be strapped for 'letting the ends run down' or for speaking to each other during the day. By three in the afternoon, the children would become drowsy and as their work slowed, the overlooker would strap them until they picked up the pace.

The children at the mill met with frequent accidents. The flies of the machines would split their knuckles as they grew tired towards the end of the day. During the two and a half years Joseph worked at the mill, about a dozen children died after leaving the mill, too tired, or too congested from the mill dust or just too crippled to work. On Saturdays, the day ended at six o'clock but they were required to settle the machines before leaving, a job that took an hour and a half. The overlookers often adjusted the clocks to make the work day longer.

When Joseph was eleven, his father Richard died, leaving the family in a desperate situation. When he was fourteen, his brother John, who was just four months short of his seventeenth birthday, lost his life after being injured at the mill. Joseph recalled John had to stop the flies with his knees because they went too fast for him to stop them with his hands. On one occasion, he bruised his shin with a spindle-board to the extent that it split open. Although the wound healed, and John was able to return to the mill, after two months, his spine was affected and he died.

Crippled by the work, Joseph needed leg irons to support him and Dr Walker ordered he wore them from ankle to thigh, but the family could not afford to have them made. The doctor gave Joseph a note, suggesting he called on a Mr Oastler and a Mr Wood. These two men were engaged in a campaign to have the Ten Hours Bill passed in Parliament and so, in exchange for his stories of his time at Bradley Mill, they gave Joseph enough money to get the braces made. Afterwards, they helped Joseph to attend school where he was able to do well and lift himself out of poverty. Joseph later told the commission: 'I worked in the factory while [till] I could work no longer; and had it not been for some friends of the Ten Hours' Bill, who sent me where I could get good support, I should have been in my grave instead of at school, where they have sent me.'

In 1833, a Factory Act was passed in Parliament, ensuring children under 9 years of age were not permitted to work in factories and those 13 or under were limited to a 42-hour work week. Joseph Hebergam eventually became a schoolmaster and married Emily Bennet, a schoolmistress, on 5 March 1850 in the Parish of Horringer in Suffolk.

Resources

During the seventeenth century and for much of the eighteenth century, children, for the most part, were not heard or even seen, despite the fact this period is now referred to as the Age of Enlightenment. The voices of Britain's poor children are all but lost in the past and it is primarily by studying the records of their parents that we can uncover their stories. One of the best resources for this period will be the parish chest records including vestry minutes, churchwardens' accounts, settlement and removal records, apprenticeship records and poor relief accounts as families sought relief from the parish.

Beginning in the nineteenth century, however, British social reformers became almost obsessed with the idea of protecting children and there is a wealth of material available in the form of first person interviews collected during the commissions convened by the government during this time. Newspapers published these accounts and many studies and books were compiled that offer an excellent insight to children in this century. Look for commissions on child labour, education and poverty both in the news and in digitized books from the period.

Children from the more affluent families are somewhat easier to trace, for wealth created its own records. Follow these children through accounts of the family, early public school records and stories of childhood reminiscence in historical magazines and books.

What type of childhood did your ancestors have?

Chapter 3

DOMESTIC AFFAIRS

'Home is where the heart is' is a saying that dates back to ancient Rome in the first century AD and has been a truism throughout all of the centuries since. Your ancestors were most likely born at home, in all probability died there as well and in between, their lives and their families centred around the place they called home.

Nowadays when we think of the environment, we generally consider the natural world as a whole, with the modern-day concerns of global warming and climate change. But for our ancestors, the environment was more local and immediate. It was both the area surrounding their home and the various aspects that contributed to their living conditions, from the physical factors of the home itself and the economic considerations of comparative wealth or poverty to the wider cultural conditions associated with urban, suburban or rural settings. Environment was the setting in the play that was our ancestors' lives, and in which they were the lead characters.

The clothes our ancestors wore in this drama included bustles and petticoats, breeches and waistcoats, shifts and corsets. Clearly, our ancestors, regardless of their position in society, were sure to have worn considerably more clothing at any one time than we do today. And yet, even the most affluent of those in the seventeenth or early eighteenth centuries would not have been able to afford the comparatively extensive wardrobes we consider essential in our time. Before the industrial age, all clothing was hand sewn and indeed even the cloth the garments were made from was laboriously woven from threads that were in turn painstakingly hand-spun. All of this hand work made the purchase of clothing an expensive proposition. For the middle classes of the late eighteenth century, the funds spent on clothing for the family might equal the rent and taxes on their home.

Whether the dwelling they inhabited was a large and sprawling country estate or a single cramped room in the basement of some city tenement, our ancestors' home was not only their residence but the place they might have found refuge and comfort. For the early working class, the home might also have been where they earned their living, either doing piecework making lace, straw hats, baskets, stockings or other small goods, providing services such as blacksmithing, butchering or barrel making, or running a small retail shop from the ground floor while living above.

Housekeeping, that is the chores involved in keeping a home such as cleaning, cooking, laundry and bill-paying, were traditionally a woman's domain. The wealthier classes employed servants for these menial chores while the working classes did for themselves and the poorest sometimes languished in filth from a lack of funds to do otherwise.

Even by the end of the seventeenth century, the majority of the land was owned by the wealthy with only a third or less held by smaller proprietors who worked their own holdings. Over the next 200 years or so, smaller holdings declined while estates grew larger through consolidation of properties, enclosure of common land and other means. For our ancestors, this meant leasing property was commonplace amongst all but the wealthiest. In some areas it was common for leases to last for a fixed number of years with twenty-one years and fourteen years both being common, and in other areas, leases were based on the lives of three named people and these types of leases were often left to our ancestors' heirs after their death.

As you imagine the domestic lives of your ancestors, try to visualize them in their homes, dressed in the common fashions and going about the business of their day. Envision their era as it really was, rather than as a still-life vignette viewed through the glass in a museum exhibit. If you are researching your family in nineteenth-century London, take a moment to smell the noxious odours wafting from the Thames and if you are studying your forebears in the seventeenth century, hear the silence of a world without machines. Only by immersing yourself in the realities of their domestic affairs will you be able to make yourself at home in their time and place.

ENVIRONMENT

Economics played a part in dictating our ancestors' environment.

Perhaps they lived in the basement of a forsaken building in one of the towns or maybe they lived in the country on an ancient estate. Whatever their circumstances, no doubt the settings in which our ancestors lived were entirely unremarkable to them as ours are to us, but certainly time and technology have served to make our world a friendlier place to live than that of our forebears. Indeed, the conditions in our ancestors' homes and workplaces would make most of us cringe in disbelief.

Unquestionably, the odours and smells of Britain's industrial past were omnipresent, less escapable and more pervasive even than the pollution of today. Raw sewage in the streets combined with unfiltered exhaust from coal fires to shroud the urban landscape of Victorian England in a choking stench. Tanneries, with their malignant reek of hides, urine and faeces. Soap works oozing a pungent odour of rotten eggs, gas and onions. Manufactories of potash spewing smoke stinking of decomposing bones. All of these and more combined to fill the towns of our ancestors with a fearsome aroma.

Ditches overflowed with sewage and filthy streets had to be flushed with water often. It was common for houses to be built with basements below the sewage pipes which resulted in waste backing up into hastily-constructed cesspits or overflowing into nearby wells meant for drinking water. And if that wasn't enough, mice and rats were commonplace in homes and workplaces, and were generally controlled by administration of poisons such as arsenic, a situation that led to more than one untimely death when the poison was accidentally consumed by family members.

The factories and workplaces of our ancestors abounded with health hazards as well. Grinders and other metalworkers in Sheffield died at an alarming rate, struck down in their prime by phthisis and other respiratory ailments caused by the dust that pervaded the unventilated workshops. In most of the textile mills of the day, workers could not see across the room as the lint from the cotton swirled in the air, coating their lungs as they breathed, and workers where often crushed in unguarded machinery. Chronic exposure to mercury produced symptoms of slurred speech, tremors and irritability in hatters. Young chimney sweeps, spending their days covered in soot, were at risk of developing cancer. Factory workers who made matches were exposed to the vapours of white phosphorus and would, over time, develop necrosis of the brain. Lead was used to make enamelware and in the manufacture of pipes to conduct water and to line cisterns, resulting in slow but steady lead poisoning with victims suffering from indigestion and then eventually paralytic symptoms leading to death.

Slowly, throughout the nineteenth century and well into the twentieth, a growing awareness of these environmental issues led to reform and various preventative laws were passed to guard public health and to clean up the worst of the industrial pollution.

Case Study – Public Health

By the mid-nineteenth century, the streets of England were full with raw sewage that ran into the rivers, mixing with sludge and chemical effluent from the manufactories, contaminating drinking water, flooding homes and spreading diseases such as cholera and typhus. This case study examines the events leading up to the Public Health Act of 1875 through accounts published both in print and in the newspapers of the time.

In London, an 1828 report from the Water Commission found the Thames was contaminated by the offal of slaughterhouses and the number of dead animals thrown into it such that there was a scum like oil floating on the surface and no fish or eels could survive even a short while in its waters. When cholera arrived in England in 1831, it spread as the sewage continued to flow into the rivers and before the disease receded, it claimed about 52,000 lives across the country. As the populations of the cities continued to swell and there was a rising awareness of the influence that poor sanitation had on the health and well-being of the citizenry. But despite the cries for reform, little was done to rectify the problem. Local authorities had little power and, for the most part, factory owners fought any proposed legislation, objecting it would interfere with their profits.

The poorest of the poor, desperate for affordable shelter, rented basements in the industrial cities, often living in crowded and unsanitary conditions. In some cases, they had no access to a privy and nowhere to discard their rubbish and in other cases, the buildings were so poorly built that the sewage and slops backed up into their living quarters. The food they purchased from unscrupulous or unknowing merchants was frequently already spoiled, with soured

'Monster Soup – Thames Water', T. McLean, c. 1828. (World Digital Library via Wellcome Library, citing Wellcome Library no. 12079i)

milk and rancid meat being all they could afford. Their drinking water often came from the very rivers that the raw sewage flowed into or from wells and cisterns equally contaminated.

Finally, in 1875, Parliament passed a Public Health Act with legislation designed to battle the growing unsanitary conditions on both land and water. Public Health Authorities were to be appointed to monitor compliance with the new laws on food, housing, water and hygiene. Medical officers were appointed to guard public health and sanitary inspectors were authorized to inspect food, ensuring it was not contaminated and had the power to order the food destroyed if it was found to be tainted. Local authorities were charged with ensuring sewers were covered, fresh water was supplied, rubbish was collected and streets were lighted. Any landlord or factory owner who did not follow the new laws could be fined and forced to clean up their properties. If a property was certified as being unfit for human habitation and was not duly put into proper tenantable repair, local authorities even had the authority to forcibly buy derelict slum buildings from their owners and demolish them.

Under the new law, it was also no longer legal for anyone to inhabit a cellar unless the ceiling height was at least seven feet and at least three feet of the seven being above ground. The cellar had to have a drain, a fireplace and an external window, and the inhabitants had to have access to a privy and an ash pit for disposal. Any newly-constructed residences had to have running water and an internal drainage system for waste water and sewage.

Despite the new laws and the authority invested in the local governments, change came slowly throughout the rest of the nineteenth century and into the twentieth century, no doubt due in a large part to the economics of such large-scale change.

Resources

Prior to the nineteenth century, local affairs were managed by the parish and so, the best resources for study of the environment of our ancestors will be the parish chest records. The vestry minutes will give details of appointments of officials while the poor and poor rate records will detail the local conditions with regards to lighting, roads, sewage, water and housing in the parish. Other records of the parish such as churchwardens' accounts, settlement records and apprenticeship records may indirectly relate to the local environment.

From the beginning of the nineteenth century, reformers concerned about the environment and public health were responsible for many inquiries and commissions on matters related to the environment and the printed accounts of these inquiries can be found in the newspapers of the time, as well as in printed journals and books. As the reformers began to gain ground with their campaigns, government studies and parliamentary debates will also contain details of local situations.

Finally, as laws were passed to protect public health and improve sanitation, remove nuisances and otherwise safeguard the environment, trial records from court cases will be good sources for further research as will the newspaper accounts of those trials.

From 1891, census records recorded the number of rooms occupied by a family if less than five. Not only can these records be used to understand the landscape of your ancestors' neighbourhood in 1891, but by locating your ancestors' addresses from earlier years in the 1891 census, you can know the number of rooms they lived in, assuming the home in question did not undergo renovations during the intervening years.

CLOTHING AND FASHION

In the early part of the sixteenth century, formal dress for Tudor men included wide-sleeved overgowns with short breeches and hose, complete with a codpiece, a look we associate with King Henry VIII. Women's fashions too were wide, with long narrow pointed bodices and very wide skirts supported by hip boulsters. The Civil War and the beheading of King Charles I marked the middle of the seventeenth century and in the aftermath the wide, imposing fashions of prior years gave way to slimmer silhouettes.

By the eighteenth century, men's clothing consisted of a longer, more fitted coat and the breeches, while still worn with hose, were longer and more close-fitting than before. For more formal occasions, men would wear the powdered wigs we associate with the period until 1795 when William Pitt imposed a tax on hair powder and the fashion quickly fell out of favour. Ladies' dresses became more elaborate, with winged cuffs and flowing skirts over stiff corsets and cane side hoops.

Hooped undergarment.

Towards the beginning of the nineteenth century, fashionable women abandoned their corsets for a time and dressed in styles reminiscent of ancient Greece and Rome, with high waists and less padding, although these styles did not last for long. Soon the ladies returned to dresses with natural waists and wide, full skirts with many petticoats. Men abandoned breeches in favour of the longer pantaloons and top hats came into fashion. By the mid- to latter part of the century, industrialization had led to new innovations in ladies' wear and the earlier petticoats and crinolines were replaced by wire frames, initially wide and full but towards the end of the century, bustles came into style. Men's suits began to look more like the suits of today, albeit with longer frock coats and slimmer trousers.

The beginning of the twentieth century saw the introduction of less formal clothing. Women slowly abandoned the corsets and crinolines of times past. Dresses grew more form fitting and hems slowly raised, showing some ankle. Men's jackets were still longer but similar in cut to those worn today and trousers were straight and occasionally cuffed. Later in the century, fashions began to change rapidly and sometimes drastically. Think of the women's miniskirts and men's beads and psychedelic clothing of the mid-1960s and imagine the reaction of your ancestors to their descendant's style of dress!

Case Study – The Trench Coat

The invention of the trench coat is claimed by two of England's nineteenth century clothing retailers. The Burberry brand, founded by Thomas Burberry in 1856, applied for a patent for the Tielocken coat in 1912 which they claim was the forerunner of the trench coat. The Aquascutum brand, founded by John Emary in 1851, began selling trench coats to the British military in 1914. Are they both right? The resources used in this case study include the company histories from their respective websites, patent records on Espacenet and historic newspapers.

Thomas Burberry was born 17 August 1835 in Betchworth, Surrey, the son of Thomas Burberry senior, a farmer, and his wife Elizabeth. After first serving an apprenticeship with master draper James Angus in Horsham, Thomas opened the original Burberry store on Winchester Street in Basingstoke in 1856, and ultimately opened a London store in 1891 at 30 Haymarket. Burberry focused on outdoor wear and outfitted explorers of the nineteenth century such as Major F.G. Jackson who mapped parts of the Arctic Circle. On 15 February 1897, Burberry filed a patent application for 'improved manufacture of Drabbet Cloth for Gabardine Fabrics'. Not only did his new weave improve the durability of the cloth but great improved its appearance

---

as well. Throughout the first decade of the twentieth century, Burberry filed for many patents related to overcoats and their materials involving improved waterproofing and construction. Finally, in 1912, he applied for a patent on the Tielocken coat. The new coat completely dispensed with buttons and instead used a single strap and buckle closure.

The founding of the Aquascutum brand is credited to John Emary, a tailor and woollen draper who had a tailor shop at 46–48 Regent Street in the 1850s. It is possible Emary may have also operated at the same address under the name Bax and Co as early as 1846, advertising in the *Morning Post* as the inventor and sole maker of the Aquascutum overcoat. Emary's son, George Moore Emary, who was 6 years old in 1856, later recalled meeting the 17-year-old Prince of Wales when he personally called at the Regent Street shop to make inquiries about the Aquascutum. In 1897, a royal warrant was received and King Edward VII himself ordered a coat in the Prince of Wales check. By 1901, the firm, now operating as Scantlebury and Commin, moved to 100 Regent Street, a location that is still the company's main showroom. It was from there the company developed the iconic trench coat in 1914, promoting the military wear with the assertion that they had specialized in waterproof coats for over fifty years.

Whether the first designer of the trench coat was Burberry or Aquascutum, history doesn't tell us, but by 1914, as the First World War began, both brands were featured in newspapers all around the country in advertisements not only for trench coats but for winter sleeping bags, campaign gloves and fleece lined service slip-ons.

Resources

When we want to know what the latest fashions in clothing are, we turn to the fashion magazines and our ancestors were no different. There are many digitized books and magazines to be found including both women's fashions and men's fashions. Look for the *Gentleman's Magazine of Fashion* from 1870 to find out what the best-dressed men were wearing and *The London and Paris Ladies' Magazine of Fashion* from 1881 for the latest styles for women.

There are also many excellent websites devoted to fashion and clothing throughout the ages. One example, Fashion-Era, has over 800 pages of fashion history rich with images, or visit the Victoria and Albert Museum website for a selection of fashions from the Victorian era. You can find other similar websites by searching for 'fashion and clothing history' in your favourite search engine.

Books are also a great resource for learning about fashions and clothing. For fashions during the era of photography, there are several books by Maureen Taylor, the Photo Detective, which will help you to date hats, bonnets, hairstyles and clothing from about 1840 onwards. Search for other books about fashion history in your local library or in bookshops.

FOOD AND COOKING

What food our ancestors ate was dependant on their economic status. The poor were thankful for whatever they could afford and often subsisted on a meagre diet of bread, butter, potatoes, beer and if they were very lucky, perhaps a little bacon or the types of meat no one else wanted, like tripe and sweetbreads. Because half of meat roasted or broiled would be lost to the fire and half of meat boiled would be lost to the water, the poor would turn what little meat they had into a broth, adding carrots, celery, turnips, cabbage, onions or leeks to stretch the meal as far as it could go, often over many days.

The wealthier of our ancestors, with more funds at their disposal, had a greater variety of food to choose from, although not the same plethora we enjoy today. Their foods were, for the most part, confined to the season although sometimes out-of-season produce might be 'forced' in the greenhouse, providing expensive treats such as early cherries and strawberries or pineapples. Upper-class dinners would most typically include a roast of venison, mutton or beef, often followed by courses of game when in season and afterwards a pastry or pudding.

Special events or occasions, such as a coronation, a military victory or the declaration of peace were sometimes marked by the gentry providing a feast for the common people in the villages surrounding their land and accounts of the fare provided are often detailed in elaborate news stories about the event. Roast beef for all, with ale a-plenty, seems to have been the standard for nineteenth-century celebrations.

Consuming tainted meat was such an ordinary occurrence that

Afternoon tea was a Victorian tradition.

during a mid-nineteenth century cholera epidemic, doctors saw fit to warn that those stricken with the disease should 'abstain from rancid meat' while ill. A certain amount of putrefaction was thought to aid in the digestion of meat but should it become too tainted, it could be rescued by boiling it for five minutes. And it was not only meat that was a concern. Many foods purchased in shops by our ancestors were either spoiled or adulterated with inedible or dangerous additives. Cayenne pepper was often cut with red oxide of lead, resulting in slow poisoning. Bread, the food of the poor, was made more cheaply by unscrupulous bakers with additives such as plaster of Paris, chalk or alum, resulting in digestive upsets for all. Some retailers, wanting to ensure the purity of their milk, added boracic acid.

The main problem, of course, was the lack of an effective way of preserving food in the days of our ancestors. Food, if not served fresh, was preserved by drying, salting, sugaring, smoking, pickling and jellying. Nuts, raisins and herbs were often dried. Vegetables were preserved in vinegar as condiments or pickles while fruits such as apricots, peaches, nectarines, apples, plums and pears were preserved with sugar, placed in a crock or jar and covered with a bladder or piece

Preserving food in jars was essential prior to refrigeration.

of leather tied with twine. Pasteurization, a very old process, was greatly improved by the French scientist Louis Pasteur in the 1860s. It was initially used as a method to preserve beer and wine, and it was not until the twentieth century that it was used for milk. Refrigeration, similarly, was initially adopted by the brewing industry, even before the slaughterhouses, and it was not until the middle of the twentieth century that residential refrigerators became common in England. By the mid-nineteenth century, tinned meat from Australia at half the price of butcher's meat was seen as an inexpensive way to feed the poor, but was not widely adopted by those who could afford the real thing.

Economic historians are not all in agreement about the effect that the Industrial Revolution had on living standards, with some saying it improved the lot of the working classes and others saying that standards fell. Still, by the second half of the nineteenth century, it is clear that relative incomes of the poor and working classes were beginning to rise while comparative food prices were falling due in a large part to improved agricultural methods. These factors combined to provide a welcome improvement to our ancestors' diets.

Case Study – Stealing to Eat

London workhouses in the early part of the nineteenth century provided the barest necessities of life. This study follows a deformed boy from the workhouse who was brought before the court on a charge of stealing. The boy claimed he stole only because he didn't have enough to eat. The resources used in this case study include newspapers and court records from the Old Bailey.

The Clerkenwell workhouse building was three storeys plus a basement and the master, Bowan, was afforded an apartment. About 500 inmates in total were housed at the workhouse, among them the poorest and most destitute of the parish.

On 6 November 1811, an inmate of Clerkenwell by the name of Edward Heath was brought before the court at the Old Bailey for having broken into the dwelling house of Thomas Bowan, the master of Clerkenwell workhouse, and stealing a sum of 240 penny pieces. Edward, at 15 years old, was crippled and depended on the workhouse for his own survival.

When Bowan discovered some of his money missing, the alarm went up and some of the coins were found in a hole under the stone staircase. An additional 30 penny pieces were found in the ward where Edward Heath had slept. When called to testify on his own behalf, Edward Heath did not try to dispute his guilt, but had offered as explanation: 'I should not have taken them if I had victuals enough; I was obliged to buy victuals every day.'

Bowen protested the inmates of the workhouse were given food enough with three-quarters a pound of bread every day and five ounces of meat on meat days. In addition, they received one ounce of cheese every day, rice mills and a full pound of rice pudding on Wednesdays.

Despite the court's observation that the boy was not particularly well fed, Heath was found guilty of stealing but not of burglary or entering the dwelling house and was sentenced to six months' imprisonment in Newgate. While there, Heath would have worn leg irons, not having the funds to pay for their removal, and would have had even less to eat than at the workhouse. Conditions in the prison were appalling and little water or food were provided to those without funds.

No doubt young Edward Heath spent the six months of his incarceration fondly remembering the starvation diet at Clerkenwell.

Resources

As anyone who has ever been trying to watch their calories knows, our generation is somewhat preoccupied with food. Advertisements, images, recipes, menus, diet plans and nutritional recommendations abound, all seeking to capture our attention and stimulate our palates. Likewise, our ancestors were perhaps similarly obsessed with food, albeit for the most part as one of the necessities of life. Look for menu plans in workhouse documents, poor relief records and society columns alike, covering diets from one end of the economic spectrum to the other.

Historical newspaper articles often featured food in some way from regular reports on imports and exports, to reviews of workhouse rations, to advertisements from retailers and even in detailed descriptions of the fare at banquets and feasts of the gentry. Search a newspaper archive for staples such as bread, wheat, oats, corn or milk either with or without a place name to find out what diets were like for your ancestors.

A number of cookbooks or cookery guides that were published throughout the eighteenth and nineteenth centuries have been digitized and are available wherever digitized books can be found. These will give a good insight into the food of the middle and upper classes, along with an appreciation of the difficulties of preserving and preparing meals without the aid of our modern appliances. Also search for farmer's guide books, books on baking, books on butchering, or even books on beekeeping to learn more about where and how your ancestors fed their appetites.

HOUSE AND HOME

In the beginning of the seventeenth century, home life generally centred in one room called the hall where the family gathered both to dine and to socialize. But towards the end of the seventeenth and into the eighteenth century, at least for those who could afford it, the dining-room where the family ate and the parlour where they socialized

Victorian era drawing room. (Wikimedia GNU free documentation licence)

became two distinct spaces within the home, with wealthier families also having a drawing room, as a place to 'withdraw' to after dinner.

In general, by the end of the eighteenth century, the standard of living had increased so even the middle-class shopkeepers and merchants lived better than their contemporaries a hundred years earlier. Their homes would have had a clock of some type, perhaps a chandelier filled with candles, an oil lamp or two, a mirror, carpets and books. Their furniture would have been in the style of Chippendale, Hepplewhite or Sheraton and they would have had knickknacks and prints on the walls. The kitchen would have been fitted with an open fireplace, fuelled by coal, with a side oven for baking bread or roasting meat. For the lower classes, the kitchen was the most important room in the house and it would have been used not only for cooking but for laundry.

The bedrooms would be found on the first or second floor and the wealthier, in addition to the bedroom, would have a closet which was used as a private office or sitting room or perhaps even a dressing room.

Victorian washstand.

Beds were typically canopied and curtained to guard against the chill. Bathrooms, of course, were non-existent and even the wealthiest used outdoor privies if they had them or if not, a chamber pot that could be emptied into a cesspit.

The poorest were often crowded into one room, and sometimes even one bed. In the rural areas, they might share their living space with livestock brought inside at night. Their belongings were few: a pot or a pan, a few wooden platters and cups, and perhaps a pewter mug; nothing more than the necessities of life.

With the nineteenth century came the spoils of the Industrial Revolution, making material goods more affordable for the middle and working classes. At the same time, rising concerns about sanitation and building standards began to improve the living spaces of even the poorest of our ancestors. Increased manufacturing and more factories generally meant the man of the house went out to work and, except for the poorest classes, the woman of the house stayed home and attended to her domestic affairs.

Did your ancestors live in a house or rented rooms? Did they live in the country, the suburbs or in a busy city street? What sort of home do you think they had?

Case Study – The Flood

On 11 March 1864, the Dale Dyke dam was breached during a storm and water swept through the Loxley Valley, through Hillsborough and into Sheffield. In the flood's path was a row of twelve cottages and shops that lined the riverside at Malin Bridge and the deluge of water washed them away, as though they were never there. One house belonged to the Price family. This case study uses newspaper accounts from the time, books about the flood and the Sheffield Flood Claims Archive website as resources.

Charles Price and his wife Elizabeth lived near Malin Bridge in the parish of Ecclesfield in a new and substantially-built cottage for which they paid a rent of £15 yearly. It was one of twelve cottages that lined the left bank of the Loxley river at Malin Bridge. The lot the Price house stood on was about 500 square yards and was held on a 99-year lease and Charles paid a yearly ground rent of £3. The property included a stable, a cow house and sheds and a large yard that was used as a coal yard and a lovely spring ran through the property. Charles Price, an earthenware dealer and general shopkeeper, was 48 years old and his wife was two years his junior. Their only son, 24-year-old Edward Dearneley Price, lived with them. Just three years earlier, Edward had married Sarah, the eldest daughter of Mr James Howe. Sarah had recently been confined and given birth to their second child and their son John Charles junior was fourteen months old.

On that Friday, 11 March 1864, there were two servants in the house along with a visitor, 17-year-old Hannah Hill from Mortomley. A relative of the Prices, Hannah had come to Malin Bridge only a few days prior to assist Sarah Price with her confinement. Unknown to the Price family, just before midnight, some eight miles away near Bradfield the earthen bank of the Dale Dyke reservoir was breached. Water, as much as 650 million gallons, began to surge down the valley in a torrent. When the great deluge of water reached Malin Bridge, the noise that accompanied it was likened by witnesses to 'a thousand steam engines letting of their steam simultaneously'. The houses near the Bridge were lifted and turned over in an instant and the entire Price family was swept away.

Young Sarah was found dead among the ruins off their road but her new-born baby, likely ripped from her arms, was never found. Sarah, along with her in-laws, were buried at Wadley as was her 14-month-old son John Charles. Edward, her husband, was not named in the burial record so presumably his body was also never found.

After the floodwater receded, nothing was left behind but slimy mud, here and there a dead animal, and the low remnants of stone walls. In the days following, a gold watch belonging to Charles Price was found buried in the mud and was given to friends of the deceased, the only reminder of the Price family to survive.

In all, about 4,000 homes were flooded and there were 240 reported deaths, although the true number who lost their lives to the devastation will never be known. So strong was the flood of water that the very course of the river had been changed as were the lives of the many people in its path.

Resources

If we know the address or the name of the home where our ancestors lived, one of the best resources to learn more about it are the local newspapers of the time. The house or property might have been advertised for auction at some point and the advertisement will give a detailed description of the property for sale, often even mentioning the current occupier and the rent paid for the home. Likewise, if the home is still extant, real estate listings may offer photographs and although a home would have changed over time, chances are, its general layout is the same. For listed buildings, search for the listing on the Historic England website to see if a description is provided.

If your ancestor's home has been torn down, you don't know the exact address or no listing information appears, you can instead learn general information about your ancestors' home by researching their neighbours' homes. Then as now, neighbourhoods tend to be home to groups of people in the same sorts of occupations and with the same economic status. Chances are your ancestor was 'keeping up with the Joneses' and their homes were remarkably alike.

Another great resource, especially in the upwardly mobile nineteenth century, are the women's magazines and digitized books on interior decorating, some with elaborate drawings and illustrations.

Even if your ancestors could not afford flocked wallpapers, mahogany panelling or damask draperies, they would have done their best to imitate the trending fashions in home décor.

HOUSEKEEPING

Despite all the modern conveniences we have today, the source of the majority of couples' arguments, after money and sex, is housework. Imagine for a moment though that cleaning the carpet meant taking it outside, hanging it between two trees and beating it with a carpet brush until your arm felt like it might fall off. What if cleaning the bathroom meant sprinkling lime or wood ashes and sawdust into an outdoor privy or emptying a chamber pot into a cesspit in a damp and mouldy cellar? Consider the ease of turning down the thermostat at night and up in the morning compared to raking the ashes out of an open hearth to save for soap-making and sifting through the coals to find those that could be reused. Measure the effort of setting the range to self-clean against the struggle and mess of blacking the hob with a mixture of charcoal and graphite. Certainly our ancestors had a much more difficult task when it came to housekeeping than we do today.

For our ancestors, doing the laundry was a multi-day event that traditionally started on a Monday. Before the advent of running water, our ancestors had to haul heavy buckets from wherever they got their water, often a communal pump or a river or stream. Next, the water had to be heated, normally in a large copper washtub, until it was as hot as could be tolerated. Soap and clothes would be added to the hot water and would be either scrubbed on a wash board or stirred and agitated with a wooden bat or dolly stick. Once the clothes were clean, they were removed and put into boiling water to kill any lice and then fished out with a laundry bat or stick.

In earlier years, our ancestors might not have used soap at all or might have used a homemade lye soap made from wood ash. By the nineteenth century, however, commercial laundry aids were more readily available and a housewife might have purchased bar soap, borax, washing soda, starch and laundry blue (a whitening agent) to make the task of cleaning the clothes a little easier.

Once the clothes had been air-dried, either outside on a clothes line or inside on a folding frame, ironing was the next step. Forged irons

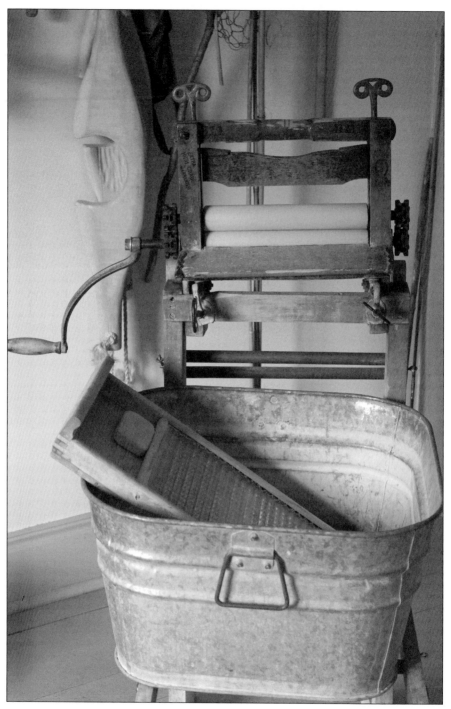

Laundry was a strenuous task for our ancestors.

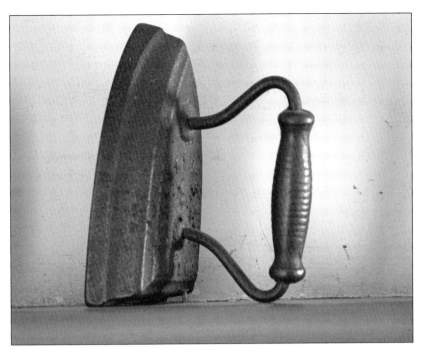

Ironing with a flat iron was hot work.

would be heated on the stove or in the fire until hot and it was the lucky housekeeper who had more than one iron so she could alternate between them. For frills and lace trimmings, a set of crimping or goffering tongs would be heated and then tested on a piece of paper to make sure they weren't so hot they would damage the delicate adornments. For a crisp finish, especially for items such as men's shirt collars, starch was used, often made from wheat flour or potatoes before commercial starch was available.

In the earliest years, straw was used to fill mattress ticks and would be changed at least once a year at harvest time. Later, feather beds and coverlets became more common although they were so valuable that in many cases, they would be specifically bequeathed to heirs in a will. They were made by saving the down and feathers plucked from fowls. The feathers were aired outside and when enough had been gathered, they were used to fill a mattress tick. Flocked beds, less common, were stuffed with locks of coarse wool or scraps of cloth. Bedsheets were used and reused, washed and re-washed until they began to wear down the middle, after which they would be turned sides to the middle or carefully patched.

While household possessions were fewer than today, keeping things clean took a great deal more effort. Cleaning was done with soap, sand, soda or linseed oil and lots of elbow grease. Crushed charcoal made a handy scouring powder, as did salt. Rugs were swept daily but rolled up and taken outdoors for a good clean from time to time. The carpet, perhaps strung between two trees on a rope, would be beaten with a stick to force the dirt and dust from the fibres.

During the winter months especially, the housekeeper was a slave to the fires, be they in the kitchen or in hearths in another room. Each day, a cloth should be laid over the carpet, if any, and the grate should be cleaned, the ashes cleared away, the hearth cleared and the fire laid anew, ready for the day. Chamber pots needed to be emptied daily into the outdoor privy or the cesspit (or in some cases, into the street) and cleaned ready for their next use.

So the next time you start to complain that it must be someone else's turn to empty the dishwasher, pause for a moment and think of the labour your ancestors put into keeping their clothes and their homes clean. Think of the hours they spent and the effort it took them and the meagre materials and tools they had to work with.

Case Study – The Housekeeper

In 1861, Mrs Beeton wrote a book about household management. In it, she details the household tasks to be done according to the season. This case study uses the 1861 edition of Mrs Beeton's guide.

During the winter, Mrs Beeton warned that there would be little time to attend to anything other than regular household duties because of the labour involved in attending to the fires in the household, although other regular duties could easily consume the entire day. In the dark months of winter, candles and lamps had to be kept trimmed and surfaces such as tables and hearths had to be scrubbed clean of smoke and soot.

The spring was the traditional time for house cleaning and removing the dirt and soot that had accumulated during the winter months from the smoke of the coal, oil or gas, no matter how fastidious the housekeeper. Before the heat of the summer, the linens

Cleaning the fireplace was a never-ending chore in the winter months.

should be washed and bleached and winter curtains should be taken down and the summer ones put up in their place. All nooks and corners should be turned out, Mrs Beeton said, and drawers, cupboards and lofts cleared of clutter. Chimneys should be swept, carpets should be taken up and cleaned, and walls should be washed and freshly coated with paint where necessary ready for the light days of the summer.

The summer, with its hotter days not conducive to hard labour, was a good time to mend the linens, patching them or turning them sides to middle. In June and July, the prudent housekeeper would preserve gooseberries, currants, raspberries and strawberries or make them into jelly or jam. With fresh vegetables readily available, mixed pickles should be put up, ready for the winter months.

Autumn was the time to preserve plums and tomato sauce and to put up pears and filberts. By October and November, the summer clothing and curtains were put away and the winter weights put back in their place. The fireplaces, grates and chimneys should be brought to readiness for the cold months ahead.

In December, she said, it was time to prepare for the Christmas season by stoning the plums, washing the currents, cutting the citron, beating the eggs and preparing the Christmas pudding ready for the feast over the holiday.

Mrs Beeton's Book of Household Management was a classic resource for Victorian women, although Isabella herself was more of a compiler than an author, since she copied most of her recipes from other sources. She unfortunately never knew quite how popular her book was to become since after the birth of her fourth child, she contracted puerperal fever and died at the age of 28.

Isabella Beeton. (Wikipedia public domain)

Resources

To learn about housekeeping in the nineteenth century, there is no better resource than *Mrs Beeton's Guide to Household Management*, highlighted in the case study. The classic book was first published in 1861 by Isabella's publisher husband Sam Beeton.

Ladies' daily journals and household accounts can be found in archive offices or sometimes scanned and digitized online. These personal accounts referring to daily activities give us a glimpse into the domestic lives of our ancestors.

From the mid-nineteenth century, cleaning products became more plentiful and were advertised in the newspapers of the times. Use various search terms in the newspaper archives and try limiting your search to advertisements to find the latest cleaning products and tools available to your ancestors.

A number of websites have been created to highlight domestic life in the past. Do a search for 'laundry history' or 'cleaning history' or 'feather tick history' or similar terms to find information online. One excellent website for this type of information, Old and Interesting, is a fascinating study of household equipment, domestic life and daily chores through the ages.

LAND AND PROPERTY

In the words of Stephen Gardiner, land is the secure ground of home, and yet for many of our ancestors, actually owning land was nothing more than a dream. That longing for a piece of the earth to call home, land that could be passed down to future generations, was no doubt the reason many chose to emigrate to one of the British colonies where their dream could be realized.

In the years after the Norman Conquest of 1066, William the Conqueror granted estates to lords who in turn forced their tenants to farm the land in exchange for a place to live, a scheme known as feudalism. After the Black Death swept through England in the fourteenth century, however, the system began to break down. The landowners who had survived the plague were desperate for labour and rather quickly, the tenants who survived the plague petitioned for freedom from their lords, choosing to pay rent in money rather than being forced to work the land of the estate. The last vestiges of feudalism were wiped out by the Tenures Abolition Act passed in 1660 after the end of the Civil War. By the 1680s as much as a third of the land was owned by small proprietors who mostly farmed their own land while the larger landlords retained control of the rest.

By the eighteenth century, the poor were gaining ground and in the new global trade market it was possible to climb out of poverty with hard work and a good business sense. The business of transferring real estate became less difficult in the Victorian era with the passage of several Acts of Parliament, including the Real Property Act of 1845 and the Conveyancing Acts of 1881 and 1882. At the same time, succession duty was imposed on freehold estates valued at over £100 in 1853, mandating that a tax be paid on property inherited after the death of the owner. Over time, this inheritance tax became a drain on the landed estates of the gentry, eventually forcing some families to sell off their properties to afford the tax. Larger properties were split into smaller ones, opening up the opportunity for the middle classes to afford to buy property. Often they would then lease the property to those less fortunate for the income the rents would provide.

Were your ancestors landowners or did they occupy the land of another? Did they struggle to pay the land taxes imposed in their time? How many in your families made the decision to emigrate to the Americas or to Australia where the land was said to be plentiful and all but free?

Case Study – Streetlam Castle Farm

Between 10 and 11 May 1787, Streetlam Castle Farm in Danby Wiske passed from William Wrightson's ownership to William Bulmer's ownership. This case study uses records of conveyance from the register of deeds, maps, probate documents and tax records to follow the land ownership in the Bulmer family over the next century.

On 10 May 1787, William Wrightson, gentleman, of Morton in the county of Durham, executed a sale contract to convey a lease on Streetlam Castle Farm to William Bulmer for one year. On the following day, 11 May 1787, Wrightson executed a release to grant William Bulmer his remaining interest. This legal manoeuvre was called a lease and release and was the most common way to convey

---

1841 tax map overlaid on Google Earth.

property from the late seventeenth century until the late nineteenth century.

The property was known as Streetlam Castle Farm or West Moor and consisted of approximately 40 acres. The land was bordered by the lane leading from Yafforth to Darlington and in 1787 it contained seven closes or fields of arable meadows and pastures.

When William died in 1825, he left the Streetlam Castle Farm property to his son Thomas: 'I give, devise and bequeath unto my son Thomas Bulmer all my real Estate and Effects of what kind soever [*sic*] lying situate and being at Streetlam in the parish of Danby Wiske and county of York.'

By the time the land was assessed for taxes in 1841, it had been divided into eleven sections including nine fields or meadows, an orchard and a garden. Thomas was renting six fields to Luke Harrison and one to John Severs, and the orchard and garden along with two fields to Christopher Metcalf.

As we can see, when each measurement was summed individually, the area of the land was 34 acres, 14 roods and 217 perches. However, there are 40 perches in a rood and 4 roods in an acre so rolling the sums up results in a total area of 38 acres, 3 roods and 17 perches. In 1841, a total of £4 4s were payable on the acreage.

When Thomas Bulmer died in 1866, he in turn left the Streetlam Castle Farm to his son Robert: 'I give and devise all my messuages or tenements lands and herditaments [sic] situated at or near Streatlam [sic – s/b Streetlam] in township of Danby Wiske in the said North Riding and County unto and to the use of my son Robert Bulmer his heirs and assigns for his sole youse [sic]'.

And so it was that Streetlam Castle Farm was passed from grandfather to father to son.

Streetlam Castle Farm 1841 Measurements Tax Record

Map	Occupier	Field	a	r	p
87	LH	East High field	3		24
88	JS	Meadow field	3	1	5
89	CM	Orchard		1	
90	CM	Garden			28
91	CM	Meadow field	5		15
92	CM	South pasture field	2	3	30
93	LH	South East ploughing field	3		10
94	LH	Little ploughing field	2	2	14
95	LH	Far middle ploughing field	4	2	28
96	LH	North Middle ploughing field	4	3	30
97	LH	Great ploughing field	8	2	33
			34	14	217

Converting the Sums to the Acreage

			a	r	p
			34	14	217
217 perches			1	1	17
14 roods			3	2	
34 acres			34		
			38	3	17

Calculating the area of Streetlam Castle Farm.

Resources

Where there was money, there were taxes and where there were taxes, there were records created. Look for tax records in the archives, even when your ancestor did not own property since chances are they leased property owned by someone else and were listed on the tax rolls as the occupier. They may even have paid the land tax themselves and claimed it back from their landlord as a rebate on their rent.

Whether your ancestors owned their own land or leased it from a land owner, they may have left probate documents that passed the land or the lease down to their heirs after their death. Where no probate document was left, you may also find letters of administration and perhaps a household inventory which can add considerably to our knowledge of how our ancestors lived.

From the late seventeenth century, look for records of lease and release on properties your ancestors might have bought and sold. As seen in the previous case study, lease and release was a common way to avoid the transfer of seisin or the title of the property. The transfer of title deeds was less common and England did not have a national registry of deeds until 1862 and even then, records are sparse since the registration was voluntary.

Newspapers are often a wonderful resource for finding detailed descriptions of properties that were being auctioned for sale. Should your ancestor have been the occupier of such a property at the time, it is quite likely they will be mentioned as the tenant, sometimes with details of their remaining lease.

If the property your ancestor owned is still extant, search for it on Google Earth and in the Listed Buildings' database if it is listed. Another excellent resource to find detailed descriptions of properties and buildings in urban areas are the fire insurance maps of the nineteenth century which can be found on the British Library website.

Chapter 4

BIRTH, LIFE AND DEATH

Our ancestors' time here on earth began with their birth and ended with their death. Between these two milestones was their life. This was hopefully spent entirely in good health, but was all too often punctuated by the traumas of illness, accident or other medical problems. In our generation, we criticize public health services, citing waiting times and treatment delays, but we certainly have it much better than our ancestors did. Not only did they have to struggle just to pay for a visit to a medical professional, but even if they managed to find the wherewithal, the practitioners of their time were only just beginning to understand how the body worked and had few resources at their disposal to treat their patients effectively.

Childbirth in the past was dangerous, both to the mother and the child. Maternal death rates as high as 5 per cent were common, even well into the twentieth century. It wasn't until the 1930s when the use of antibiotics finally reduced the number of maternal deaths from puerperal pyrexia, haemorrhage, convulsions and occasionally illegal abortion. Infant mortality was likewise a high risk with as many as 170 deaths per 1,000 live births being recorded in England before 1900.

For infants who survived childbirth, their chance of a healthy life was complicated by many factors. For some, economic circumstance meant their diet was poor and for others, their environment took a toll on their health but overall, our ancestors just had less knowledge of what was good for them and what was not. The dangers of substance abuse had yet to be discovered and the benefits of nutritious food, clean water and clear air, while perhaps suspected, were not given the same consideration they are today.

Not only did the medical community collectively have far less knowledge of human physiology than today, but there was little understanding of factors that contributed to mental health problems

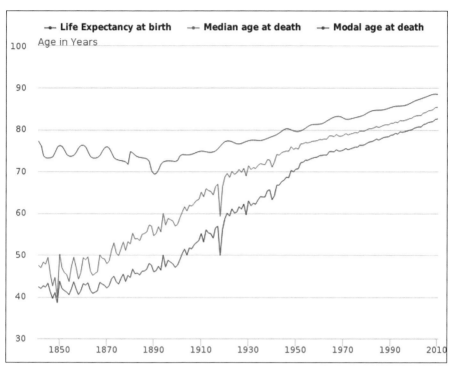

Age at death for females 1841 to 2010. (Office for National Statistics)

Age at death for males 1841 to 2010. (Office for National Statistics)

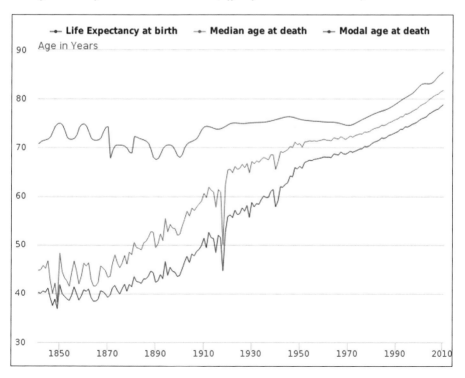

and no medicines, treatments or diagnostic measures to deal with the frequent outbreaks of disease. Epidemics emerged sporadically, paying little respect to class or social standing, and took their victims from all walks of life.

Our ancestors expected to live only a fraction of the years we regularly attain. Although the lack of centralized record-keeping makes it difficult to ascertain, many historians estimate by the end of the eighteenth century, the average life expectancy was only about forty years, and although it continued to rise throughout the nineteenth century as average incomes rose, sanitation improved and medical knowledge increased, our ancestors did not routinely expect to live a long life.

As we move back in time to visit with our ancestors, we find that the circle of birth, life and death was surely a much smaller one, both delicate and fragile. Their lives began at home, were lived at home and frequently ended at home. Until the twentieth century when hospitals and undertakers began to intrude, birth and death, the most vital of life's events, were personal and took place at home with family in attendance.

Certainly, our ancestors were no strangers to death. Losing siblings, parents and spouses in untimely ways was all too common. And even while death was sometimes expected, it did not lessen their grief. They mourned deeply, often publicly, adopting mourning dress and observing the rituals of bereavement. They sought solace in religion and found comfort in the outward symbols of death and a belief in the afterlife as they buried their loved ones.

Just like our generation, our ancestors began the walk towards death from the moment of their birth, but unlike our generation, their pace was often hurried along by uncontrollable influences prevalent in their time and place. By the conclusion of this chapter, you will have a better understanding of challenges your ancestors faced and how those milestone dates of birth, marriage and death on your pedigree charts framed your ancestors' lives. You will be able to start sketching in details and perhaps even begin colouring in their portraits with your social history research.

BIRTH

There is probably not a genealogist among us who does not have at least one family (and probably several) where one or more of the children born didn't survive their first year of life. What we can't know, in most cases, is how many more of our ancestors' children were stillborn, never even having the opportunity to take their first breath. Registration of stillbirths was not a requirement in England and Wales until 1926 or in Scotland until 1938. Clues may exist in the form of gaps between living children but more than likely, there will be no evidence left to mark the sad event.

Other times, it was the baby who survived, with the mother succumbing to either puerperal pyrexia (more commonly known as childbed fever) or another maternal affliction. These cases are easier to identify and we will often find a record of a child's birth followed a few days later by the death of its mother. Husbands, faced with their wife's untimely death and with having a newborn baby and perhaps other small children to care for, often found themselves in an untenable position. On the one hand, they had to work to provide for their family, but on the other hand, they had to stay home to look after them. If the bereaved father was fortunate, some other family member was able to step in and give aid, but for others, the only solution was to find another wife as soon as possible. As social historians, we need to step into our ancestors' lives to understand the pressures they faced and understand the rapidity of remarriage was out of necessity rather than seemingly callous behaviour.

Before the nineteenth century, expectant mothers were most often attended by close female relations or friends in their homes, and perhaps assisted by the local midwife. Although the first lying-in hospital was opened in London in 1767, maternity hospitals were not common until much later. From about the beginning of the nineteenth century, childbirth was beginning to be seen as a problem, one that required fixing, and doctors began to intrude into the affair, pushing aside the family and midwives. With this intrusion, however, ironically came a much higher instance of maternal death from childbed fever since the idea of clean hands and sterilized medical instruments did not really gain a foothold until well into the second half of the nineteenth century thanks to the research of Joseph Lister.

Childbirth was not only dangerous for both the mother and the child, it also happened more often since our ancestors typically had more children than families do in our time. While the average woman in England today has had 1.9 children by the time she is 45 years old, our ancestors' families might have averaged five or six children per family back in 1810 and 1820, and larger families than that were quite common.

Did your ancestors have large families? Were there gaps in the years of their children's births? Did they lose children at an early age? Did any of them remarry hastily after the death of a spouse? Look at the records of your family tree for these answers, but don't forget to look beyond the records for a deeper understanding of your ancestors' challenges.

Case Study – Manslaughter in Childbirth Death

When Betty Kay went into labour in Great Bolton, Lancashire on 12 July 1830, she was attended by one James Ferguson, man-midwife. Within less than a day of giving birth, Kay was dead and on 25 August, Ferguson was found guilty of manslaughter at the Lancaster Assizes. This case study looks at accounts of the events which were published in the newspapers of the time as well as using traditional genealogical resources.

Two weeks before Betty Kay's expected confinement, her husband John, a poor weaver of Bolton, made arrangements with James Ferguson to attend his wife when the time came. For his services, Ferguson demanded a fee of 5s 6d but agreed to accept a note given to Betty from the Lying-in Charity for 3s 6d as partial payment.

Although James Ferguson's two brothers, John and Fergus, were respected surgeons in Bolton, James had no formal medical education and primarily earned his living as a weaver. For a time in his youth, he had thought to become a surgeon, apprenticing with his brother John for seven years, but he had not taken a diploma nor did he have any authority for practising. Although the 30-year-old Ferguson had given up medicine to become a weaver, from time to time he would still attend poor women in their confinements.

Betty Kay went into labour early on the morning of Sunday, 11 July and her mother, Margaret Kay, arrived at the Kay's cottage at about 7 o'clock, accompanied by Mary Longworth, a family friend who had considerable experience with childbirth. Shortly after their arrival, Ferguson was sent for. He arrived at 8 o'clock and within an hour and a half, the child was delivered.

After the baby's delivery, Ferguson told John Kay that Betty was doing well but the afterbirth would take time to come and he would leave and return in a while. It was not until 1 o'clock that afternoon when Ferguson, much the worse for drink, arrived back at the Kay cottage. When Ferguson went up to see Betty, he found her bleeding heavily, but soon came down, again telling the husband the afterbirth had still not come but it would, eventually. He left then and returned about 6 o'clock in a yet even more intoxicated state. Seeing Betty's condition was worse, he asked Kay for money with which to buy medicine and left again, saying he would return once he had purchased it. When Ferguson finally came back at 9 o'clock with the medicine, he was very drunk.

When the afterbirth still had not come and by 11 o'clock that night, Betty Kay, fearing she was dying, urged her husband to fetch another doctor. Kay went to Ferguson's brother, a surgeon, but he refused to come, saying he had been estranged from his brother James for more than a decade.

After more than fifteen hours of extensive haemorrhaging, Betty Kay died in the early hours of the next morning, just after half-past 12. Her body was examined by Dr John Marshall Robinson and his brother Richard Robinson, both surgeons at Bolton. Robinson found the patient had died from exsanguination due to the haemorrhaging caused by the afterbirth that had never been delivered. In his opinion, the death could have been prevented had the afterbirth been removed. James Ferguson was indicted for manslaughter.

At the trial, the defence called into evidence the recommendations of Dr Hunter who was a Surgeon at the Lying-in Hospital in London, citing his belief that the afterbirth be delivered naturally, and it could take as long as 24 hours to come. Dr Robinson, on re-examination noted that although Hunter had been an eminent surgeon, it had been 30 years since he had practised but he himself had attended about 600 patients in childbirth in the course of a year and had lost only one or two. It was his own opinion if there was haemorrhage, the afterbirth should be taken away by the practitioner.

John Kay, Margaret Kay and Mary Longworth all testified James Ferguson had been drunk much of the day and he had refused to deliver the afterbirth. Witnesses for the defence were Ellen Wood and Betty McCree, and they contradicted the Kay's testimony, saying they did not see Ferguson in a state of intoxication and he had suggested taking the afterbirth but the deceased had refused to let him. After hearing all the evidence, his lordship instructed the jury that the question at hand was whether the accused had caused the death of Betty Kay through gross ignorance and neglect. Whether the accused was intoxicated should not be considered, he told them, since there was conflicting testimony from the witnesses.

After only a few moments' deliberation, the jury found Ferguson guilty of manslaughter by careless and unskilful treatment of the deceased. His Lordship sentenced Ferguson to six months' imprisonment in Lancaster Castle, saying he did so as a deterrent to others who might act in the same manner under similar circumstances.

Resources

After July 1837, finding our ancestors' birth records is usually easily achievable. Births were registered with the General Register Office (GRO) and certificates are available from them for a fee. Information on a birth record includes where they were born which is most often the home address, the names of the parents, including the mother's maiden name, the father's occupation and who registered the birth and when. If the birth was registered by the mother soon after the infant's birth, it is reasonable to assume there were no complications. If the birth took place somewhere other than at the home address, there may have been concerns about the mother's health or the impending delivery.

Prior to July 1837, the first record in a child's life is usually the baptism record, most often in the local parish church registers. The information contained in a baptism entry varies significantly over time and depending on the parish. From 1813, when pre-printed baptism record books were mandated, the record will contain the baptism date, the names of the child and the parents, the place of abode and the occupation of the father. Often times, when the birthdate was known, it would be recorded on the side of the entry. Prior to 1813, the baptism records are a mixed bag but many contain only the most basic information of baptism date with only the name of the child, the father and sometimes the mother. Many parish records have been microfilmed or digitized over the last few decades. Some can be found online on

Family Search, Ancestry, Findmypast or The Genealogist while others are held by county record offices or other archives.

When looking at baptismal records, watch for notations that the baptism was private. This can sometimes mean the child being baptized was not expected to survive, and the baptism had to be done quickly, at the home of the parents. Normally, baptism was performed in the church on the Sunday following the birth or the Sunday after that. Sometimes the infant was taken to the clergyman's house within a few days of birth. A later baptism might suggest the mother had a difficult birth or it might just be that baptism was not a priority for the family. Look at the interval for the parent's other children and for the children of the other parishioners.

From the beginning of the nineteenth century, look for medical journals that might describe specific maternity cases or detail statistics for a particular region and time as a general reference. The *British Medical Journal* from 1840 has been digitized and is accessible from many libraries and can be found on jStor while other journals such as *The Lancet* are available on Google Books.

HEALTH AND LIFESTYLE

One thing is probably certain. Our generation spends more time considering whether our lifestyle is a healthy one than our ancestors ever did. In fact, the very term 'lifestyle' as we know it, was only coined in 1929 by the psychologist Alfred Adler. Where many in our time avidly read the latest exercise advice looking for the magic bullet, most of our ancestors probably only thought about rest and relaxation as they laboured, sweated and even bled to earn a living for themselves and their families.

Also unlike our generation, our ancestors most likely did not choose to eat an unhealthy diet laden with carbohydrates and little protein, but many were forced to out of economic necessity. They could not pick from the wide variety of foods we find in our supermarkets, and instead had to grow their own produce, raise their own meat, milk their own cows and bake their own bread. They did not worry about how many calories they consumed because there were seldom enough when measured against the physical labour they had to do daily.

From the end of the eighteenth century, however, as industrializ-ation swept the country, suddenly there were machines to do the hard

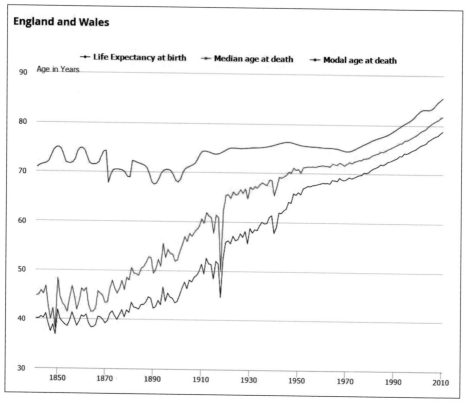

England and Wales

Life expectancy 1840 to 2010. (Office for National Statistics)

work and the heavy lifting. Slowly, our ancestors began transitioning from working physically hard every day, to monitoring machines, managing people and pursuing the dream, but the poor still laboured in low-paying and dangerous jobs in the factories that sprung up throughout the nineteenth century. Working conditions were far more hazardous than they are today, with our increased focus on health and safety. Long working hours, poorly-guarded machines and exposure to noxious chemicals led to many factory accidents, injuries and even death.

Poor diets, contaminated water, long working hours and dangerous occupations all took their toll on our ancestors' health, making them more susceptible to the myriad of diseases that threatened lives in their time. Tuberculosis, cholera, smallpox, measles, scarlet fever and whooping-cough all took more victims from the industrialized cities and towns in the nineteenth century than from the rural population who were more likely to have clean water and a better diet.

According to a report published by the Office for National Statistics, life expectancy is still higher today for those living in rural communities, suggesting that although the health and lifestyles of our generation have improved over those of our ancestors, we are probably much better served by going out to work in the garden than by heading to the gym.

Case Study – The Bicycling Craze of the 1890s

Before the dawn of the industrial age, our ancestors laboured from sunrise to sunset just to keep food on the table and a roof over their head. But as more of our ancestors left their rural villages for the new factory jobs in the cities, they assumed more sedentary lifestyles, setting the stage for the bicycle craze of the 1890s. This case study examines the rise in popularity of the bicycle using general history resources and newspaper articles from the period.

In the early 1860s, the first true bicycle was invented in France and by 1868, the velocipedes, as the cycling machines were called, were being mass-produced throughout Europe. Throughout the next decade, the design of the English bicycle began to change and the front wheel became considerably larger than the rear wheel. This design became known as the 'penny-farthing' since the ratio of the diameter of the front wheel to the back wheel of the bicycle were like the ratio of the penny coin to the farthing coin. While these early bicycles were popular with the rich young gentlemen who could afford them, most people thought they were not only too expensive but very dangerous as well. With riders sitting high atop the wheels, riding along at speed often ended with the rider coming off the bicycle, resulting in broken bones or even fatalities.

That all changed in the 1890s with the invention of the safety bicycle. The gear ratios of the new design allowed the front and back wheel to be the same size and much smaller, and thanks to the lower design, riders could reach the ground with their feet, making stopping easier and cycling generally much safer. Acceptance grew and cycling clubs were viewed with approval by not only the general public, but even by the church, with Rev W. J. Dawson of Yorkshire

---

declaring that in ten years' time, there 'will probably be scarcely a youth with a proper sense of life in him who will not ride'.

Some of the older generation still thought cycling was for men only, but as time went on, more women learned to ride, making the necessary adjustments in their clothing. Cycling clubs sprang up all around the country, some exclusively for women cyclists or 'wheelwomen', such as the Mowbray House Cycling Association established in 1893. Its members were primarily women of the upper classes and one of the supporters was Frances Evelyn 'Daisy' Grenville, the mistress of Albert Edward, the Prince of Wales, who inspired the song 'Daisy, Daisy', the lyrics of which ended with 'a bicycle built for two'. The club members, when not cycling, devoted their time to raising money to buy bicycles for working women who could not afford to buy their own. By the end of the decade, the number of women-only cyclist clubs was at an all-time high and the latest fad for ladies' cycles in 1897 was a bouquet-holder for flowers, fixed in the centre of the handlebars.

Although many bicycle clubs folded early in the twentieth century as the automobile began to take centre stage, by then, the bicycle was an established mode of transport for many and is still a popular form of recreation and exercise today.

Resources

Researching our ancestors' health and lifestyle is a challenge, not because resources are lacking but because there are too many, although none are specific or definitive unto themselves. Instead, we need to examine all the very specific genealogical records that relate to our ancestors and put together a timeline of their lives so we can turn to more general social history resources for an understanding of what effect their particular circumstances might have had on their health and on their lifestyle.

To create a timeline for your ancestor, make a list of all the events in their life. When and where was your ancestor born? When and where did they get married? When and where did they die? Did you find the family listed in any census records or city directories? What sorts of occupations did the family have? Did they leave a will? Put all the relevant details into date order in a document or spreadsheet and use the events in the lives of their family to add further details to their timeline.

Some of the records used to construct the timeline will have specific information about the health of your ancestors. Death certificates will give cause of death which can give us an understanding of a person's health in the latter stages of their life. Wills sometimes mention the physical and mental health of the testator, the person who wrote the will, with statements such as 'being infirm of Body but of Perfect and sound Memory Thanks to God' being common, and might even allude to the health of others mentioned in the will, such as when an heir is bequeathed an inheritance on the condition of caring for another ailing

Use Excel to plot your ancestors' ages at death.

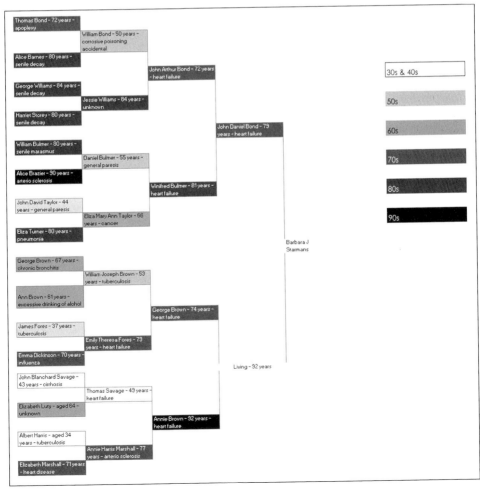

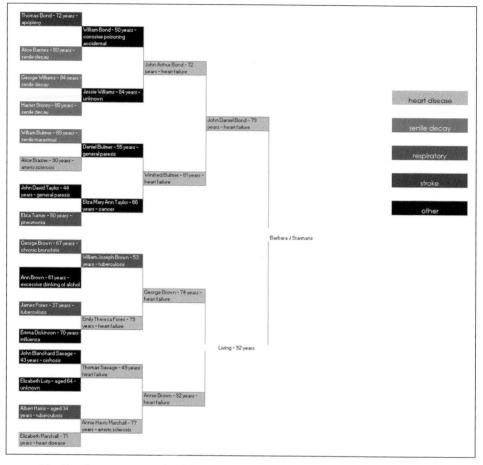

Use Excel to create a medical family tree.

family member for their lifetime. Few parish register burial records mention cause of death, but some do and it is worth consulting the original records just in case.

The constructed timeline should also be used to do more general research into the health and lifestyles of your ancestor and their contemporaries in newspapers, books and published reports that give details of the health, economic status and lifestyle of the population of a particular neighbourhood or of those who worked in your ancestor's specific occupation. In particular, reports of various Royal Commissions throughout the nineteenth century give a wealth of detail about the lifestyles of our ancestors who lived in the places where the commission was conducting its inquiry or who worked in the occupation that was being researched by the commissioners. In addition, parish chest records such as churchwarden accounts, poor rate records and vestry minutes might also give similar details.

MEDICINE

At the beginning of the nineteenth century, medical professionals were divided into three specialties: physicians, surgeons and apothecaries. Young men of means attended Oxford or Cambridge to become physicians and were given positions in the best hospitals in London, serving mostly the upper-class elite. All other classes of patients generally made do with a surgeon or an apothecary for medical care. Aspiring surgeons and apothecaries usually entered into an apprenticeship to receive both theoretical and practical training from a master although there was little oversight in either profession and not all masters were equally qualified. The three branches of the medical profession were governed by the Royal College of Physicians, the Company of Barber-Surgeons and the Worshipful Society of Apothecaries.

The Apothecaries' Act, passed in 1815, introduced formal qualifications with mandatory five-year apprenticeships for apothecaries and is viewed by many as the beginning of regulation in the medical profession. The Medical Act of 1858 was introduced to further regulate the qualifications of practitioners in Medicine and Surgery and although it recognized the individual companies, it also established the General Medical Council. The Council was responsible to Parliament and not only maintained the new Medical Register which was a public list of all recognized medical practitioners, but also defined what the qualifications were for registration.

For our ancestors, medical care before the passage of the 1815 and 1858 Acts was very much a hit-and-miss affair. While some practitioners were no doubt learned men of much experience in the medical knowledge of the day, others were nothing more than quacks and charlatans, pretending to possess the knowledge to heal, but who did far more harm than good with their often ineffectual and sometimes dangerous treatments. The early medical practitioners were patronized and judged, not on their knowledge of medicine, but on whether they effected a cure. No doubt there were many cases where patients were reportedly healed by a tincture or concoction or treatment who would

Speed was more important than skill when it came to amputations.

have recovered from their ailment or injury just as quickly without any medical intervention.

The regulation provided by the medical Acts, combined with clinical training, education and an increased understanding of the workings of the human body, gave rise to a more well-rounded medical professional, one who was knowledgeable in medicine, surgery, midwifery, chemistry and pharmacology. This new breed of medical man brought their services to the middle classes, particularly in the middle and north of England. Eventually even the London physicians began to support the system and new regulations as more of them were exposed to training in the clinical practices typically followed in both Scotland and France.

By the latter part of the nineteenth century, our ancestors were more likely to consult a medical professional for their health problems than they were to rely on home remedies or back-alley cures. They were probably likewise more prone to visit the apothecary or chemist's shop to get advice on the latest medications, rather than pop around to the local shop for a bottle of tonic or elixir.

Are you aware of any of your ancestors who sought medical

treatment? Were they ever in hospital or under the care of a medical man? Examine the death certificates of your ancestors to see if the informant was a family member or a medical professional.

Case Study – The London Smallpox Hospital

Revolutionary in its time, the London Smallpox Hospital was opened in 1745, not only to treat those with smallpox, but also to research prevention and treatments. This case study looks at the important role this hospital played in London's healthcare using general history resources and journal articles from the period.

In 1746, when the London Smallpox Hospital in Coldbath Fields opened its doors to patients, it was the only hospital of its kind in Europe. Supported by subscriptions made by the noble and wealthy classes, it offered care to smallpox victims of both sexes and of all ages, providing them with medical attention and a suitable diet during their illness. At the same time, medical practitioners in Lower Street, Islington, were experimenting with inoculation, a process that infected people with a mild and manageable form of smallpox that would protect the patient from contracting a more virulent smallpox infection in the natural way.

Physicians and surgeons were not paid for their work in the hospital and were expected to support themselves in private practice. Neither were the administrators, apothecaries, messengers, matrons or nurses allowed to take any payment or gratuity from the patients. All revenue was raised by subscription or charitable donations, with those who donated the most being afforded a vote in the management of the hospital. In addition, all annual subscribers were entitled to one bed in the hospital for themselves, their family or their friends.

One of the most unusual aspects of the new Smallpox Hospital was that it would treat anyone who had the disease, or anyone who wanted to be inoculated, without fee or recommendation. Eight times a year, a notice would be given that people wishing to be inoculated would be received in Islington. Once applications had been made, a letter would be sent to the applicants letting them know when they could be admitted for the procedure. Those patients who already had smallpox and wanted to be admitted to the Coldbath Fields site were required to provide a deposit of £1 and 6 pence to cover the cost of their burial. Should they recover from the disease, this deposit would be refunded on discharge. No visitors were allowed, to make sure the disease was not spread, and while in the hospital, the smallpox sufferers were given clothing to wear so their own could be fumigated with brimstone (sulphur).

The London Smallpox Hospital brought London through the many smallpox epidemics of the eighteenth and nineteenth centuries and was instrumental in perfecting Dr Edward Jenner's practice of vaccinating people with cowpox to protect them from smallpox. Over the years, the location and name of the hospital changed and in the twentieth century it was made part of the Whittington Hospital NHS Trust.

How many of our ancestors were saved, either by being treated at the hospital, or by being inoculated or vaccinated against the horrible ravages of smallpox using methods developed by the research done there?

Resources

It is unfortunate that often the only time we can know our ancestors suffered from medical conditions is when they ultimately died from them. If all went well when they sought the care of a physician, purchased medications from an apothecary or went under the knife of a surgeon, there is unlikely to be a record of the event. But logically, we know they must have at least suffered from many of the same minor ailments as we do. The common cold and the stomach flu are not a twenty-first century invention. Look for medical journals or newspaper reports describing the diseases common in a time and place. These often discuss the latest treatments and their success rates.

Although at first consideration it seems unlikely old medical records are still extant, don't discount finding hospital records for your ancestors. The National Archives website, in partnership with the Wellcome Library, has a database of which hospital records survive, what they contain and where they are located. While many records are only administrative in nature, a few patient files from our ancestors do still exist but be aware that records less than 100 years old are normally sealed for privacy reasons.

Like us, our ancestors most likely availed themselves of the services and facilities that were convenient to their homes. Examine maps contemporary to the time of your ancestors to find out if there was a hospital or an infirmary in their area and check commercial directories for apothecary shops, surgeons or physician's offices in your ancestors' neighbourhoods. Search local newspapers for further clues to what medical professionals operated in the area and what they specialized in.

DISEASES AND EPIDEMICS

Any genealogist who has spent time reading through parish registers knows the sadness that overwhelms them when they reach a point in the registers where suddenly the burials just seem to run on for pages. These unmistakably tragic periods in a parish's history are most often indicative of an epidemic of a particular disease that killed many parishioners over a short period. Perhaps it was the plague, maybe it was smallpox or possibly it was cholera, but whatever the case, there probably wouldn't have been anyone left in the area who did not mourn for a friend, neighbour or family member.

Today, the leading causes of death are lung cancer, respiratory diseases and stroke but in our ancestor's time, they died mainly from other diseases that are far more treatable in our generation. The leading cause of death in the mid-nineteenth century was tuberculosis, also called consumption, phthisis or scrofula. Known as the 'romantic disease' for the 'slow death' it caused, tuberculosis found an increasing number of victims throughout the nineteenth century, spreading from person to person in the poorest and most crowded neighbourhoods of the industrial cities.

Next to tuberculosis, our forebears often fell prey to dysentery, or the bloody flux as it was sometimes called, a widespread disease in consequence of the unsanitary conditions that prevailed in our ancestors' era. These same unwholesome conditions were also later found to be responsible for the rapid spread of cholera during the global pandemics that swept the world time and time again during the nineteenth century.

Another killer, the waterborne bacterial infection known as typhoid fever, took the life of Prince Albert, the beloved husband of Queen Victoria, when he was only 42 years old, leaving her in mourning for the rest of her life. Typhoid fever was responsible for countless deaths between 1846 and 1849 during the potato famine in Ireland and it was so widespread in prisons throughout England that it was also frequently called gaol fever.

With few effective treatments for these killer diseases other than rest and palliative care, epidemics of tuberculosis, dysentery, cholera, typhoid, diphtheria, scarlet fever, meningitis, measles and whooping-cough headlined the mortality rolls in turn in various locales during the time of our ancestors, frequently following negative socioeconomic influences such as wartime, economic depression, unemployment, rising food prices, famine, poor sanitation and urban overcrowding.

Our ancestors must have lived in fear of the epidemics and diseases of their time. They sometimes fled their homes, towns and villages in search of refuge while other times they stood their ground armed with little more than superstition and folk remedies. How often did disease and epidemic illnesses strike your families and leave them with heart-breaking losses to bear?

Case Study – Scarlet Fever and the Economy

Throughout the latter half of the nineteenth century, scarlet fever deaths in England reached epidemic levels every five to six years claiming many thousands of young lives. This case study considers the possible relationship between peaks in deaths due to scarlet fever and peaks in the price of wheat using a scientific study discussed in a book from Cambridge University Press and newspaper articles from the time while profiling a specific family who suffered a series of tragic losses including the death of a child from scarlet fever.

In 1815, Parliament introduced restrictions and significant tariffs on imported grain to try to stimulate domestic production. This legislation, referred to as the Corn Laws, did indeed raise the price of domestic grain, benefitting the farmers in the rural districts but adversely affected the working man who struggled to afford bread, the most basic of foods. Over the following two decades, opponents

---

of the tariffs fought to repeal the Corn Laws and in 1838, the Anti-Corn Law League was formed. With good harvests in 1844, the protests abated but the poor harvests of 1845 in combination with the potato famine in Ireland finally led to repeal of law and the tariffs in a series of gradual reductions spread over three years.

On 25 November 1845, Caroline Storey married Charles Henry Leek in the Parish Church of Newchurch on the Isle of Wight. Within a few months, Caroline was with child and on 8 October 1846, she gave birth to fraternal twins, a boy and a girl. Little Harriet, the girl, lived only four months, dying on 22 February 1847 from a birth debility. That same year, towards the beginning of October, Charles Leek developed pneumonia and after a seven-day battle, he died at home on 13 October, his father George in attendance. In reduced circumstances, Caroline struggled to provide for young Walter, sharing her burden with her brother-in-law Henry Leek as the two ran a bath chair hire business from their home on Pier Street near the harbour in Ryde. Then on 25 October 1851, the unthinkable happened, and Caroline's five-year-old son Walter came down with scarlet fever and died. Within five short years, Caroline had lost her husband and both her children and was no doubt wondering why fate had been so cruel.

But according to a study on the dynamics of the scarlet fever epidemics that swept England repeatedly between 1847 and 1880, deaths from the outbreaks could be correlated to the oscillation in wheat prices, although with a lag of two or three years. The study suggested the high wheat prices and the resulting inadequate nutrition of both pregnant mothers and small children had a very direct impact on the deaths attributable to scarlet fever in the years that followed.

The repeal of the Corn Laws and the subsequent fall in the prices of grain and the corresponding increase in the availability of food came too late for Caroline Leek whose tragic losses must have haunted her until her death in 1891 at the age of 82.

Resources

One of the best resources for finding out about local disease outbreaks and epidemics are the historic newspapers for your ancestors' time and place. Officials often reported on the status of outbreaks and on their efforts to contain them. Mortality statistics and the numbers of people infected were usually reported regularly for the duration of the epidemic.

For more in-depth information on diseases and their spread, treatment and mortality rates, search for medical journals, research papers and case studies written by the medical practitioners of your ancestors' time and place. The *British Medical Journal* is one of the oldest general medical journals, first published in 1840 as the *Provincial Medical and Surgical Journal*. Access various editions of the journals on Google Books, Internet Archive and on jStor through your local library.

Also of interest to social historians researching diseases and epidemics are the London Bills of Mortality which originated in the sixteenth century. Early bills from 1664 and 1665 have been digitized and are available at the Wellcome Library website and the Internet Archive has a collection of the Yearly Bills of Mortality from 1657 to 1758 in book format. Beginning in the eighteenth century, the bills were also published in the London newspapers.

There are also a great many books, both digital and print, that describe the diseases that were the scourge of previous generations. Search Google Books, the Internet Archive or World Cat to find resources to study. There have also been many scholarly research papers written on the topic, ranging from statistical analysis to more detailed medical studies and to the impact of epidemics on the communities of our ancestors' era.

MENTAL HEALTH

In our ancestors' time, mental health issues were poorly understood. Those who suffered from depression, schizophrenia, bipolar disorders and anxiety would often be physically restrained, abused and hidden away in a dark room or in one of the asylums that opened in increasing numbers after the beginning of the nineteenth century.

Bedlam, perhaps the earliest and most infamous asylum in England's history, opened just outside the walls of London in 1247 as the Priory of the New Order of St Mary of Bethlem, a haven for the poor. When it first became a home for the insane is not known but it is thought this was in the latter part of the fourteenth century. By at least the beginning of the seventeenth century, the public were actually encouraged to visit to be entertained by the deranged and mentally-disturbed inmates and the fees collected from the visitors were put towards the maintenance of the hospital. Bedlam, as it was by then known, was very much a tourist destination, just like the London Bridge or the Tower of London. By the end of the eighteenth century, the building was beginning to show its age, with heaving floors and crumbling walls, and in 1815, the inmates were moved to a new building near Lambeth Road. But, despite the new building, the mentally ill were still referred to in derogatory terms such as mad, deranged and lunatics, and were generally not well treated.

About this same time, there was a growing public awareness that many of the mentally ill had nowhere to go. The numbers of patients housed in asylums and madhouses went from about 10,000 at the beginning of the nineteenth century to nearly ten times as many at its conclusion. Some were sent to private houses for care where the circumstances ranged from barely acceptable to unimaginable and horrific. With few alternatives, these private houses became increasingly common. Admission was based on the ability of the family to pay for the keeper's services and discretion rather than the need of the patients.

Paupers were sent to public asylums, which were often severely overcrowded and as a result, most suffered horribly from neglect and poor nutrition. The majority of the poor left the asylums in coffins, rather than being cured and discharged. But whether the patients found themselves in private care, or in county hospitals such as Bedlam or the York Lunatic Asylum, they often suffered not only from neglect, but also from mistreatment and cruelty. This general abuse became so widely known that the government introduced a series of Acts beginning with the 1828 and 1832 Madhouse Acts that sought to regulate homes that cared for the mentally ill. These new regulations, combined with new and innovative treatments promoted by reformists in mental health slowly began to change the situation for those suffering from mental illness.

Case Study – The York Retreat

Prior to the beginning of the nineteenth century, our ancestors with mental health issues were treated abominably, sometimes left naked, chained and isolated. The York Retreat facility, opened in 1796, introduced new humane and morally acceptable methods of treatment, inspiring a change in attitudes towards mental illness that eventually spread around the globe. This case study looks at the events that led up to its inception, using books, genealogy records and newspapers from the time.

Hannah Mills was a young Quaker from Hunslett Carr in Leeds. Her weaver husband Samuel died in 1787 and finding herself widowed at an early age, Hannah sunk into what we would now understand was a deep clinical depression. She was eventually admitted to the York Asylum, and it was said she suffered from melancholy. When her friends and family tried to visit her at the asylum, they were refused and told Hannah was in private treatment and could not be disturbed. Then, only a few weeks after her admittance, Hannah died.

After her death on 29 April 1890, Hannah's Quaker Friends were distrustful of what the asylum staff told them about how Hannah had died and wanted to uncover the truth. Friend William Tuke, a tea dealer, along with Godfrey Higgins, a magistrate and land owner, were asked to investigate the conditions at York on behalf of the community. What they found there appalled them. Inmates were kept in horrifying conditions, tortured with violent purges, sudden cold baths and other inhumane treatments.

In reaction to this, Tuke conceived the idea of the York Retreat, a facility run by Quakers, for the care of Quakers who suffered from mental illness. When the Retreat opened its doors on 11 May 1796, it was largely due to William Tuke who had solicited annuities, donations and annual subscriptions from the Quaker community to build the facility that could care for about thirty patients at a time. Treatments used were gentle. The patients wore their own clothes and were encouraged in quiet and thoughtful pursuits. Rather than being tortured into submission, they were allowed to walk in the grounds surrounding the retreat and to do farming chores and other tasks to keep their bodies occupied while their minds healed. Many

The original building of the York Retreat, c. 1796. (Wikimedia, public domain)

of the patients so treated were indeed cured and were discharged to go on and lead full lives outside of the institution.

By the latter half of the nineteenth century, the Quaker influence on the Retreat had diminished and most of the patients were no longer Friends but the changes in public perceptions of mental illness and the new approaches to care and treatment lived on and were expanded upon in facilities all around the world.

Resources

In the twenty-first century, we are exceptionally concerned about privacy and many recent laws, rules and regulations have been enacted to make sure our personal information is guarded, especially in the area of medical records. We are bombarded daily with terms such as privacy, consent, data protection and permission and are often asked to fill in permission forms both to allow collection of and to grant access to our personal information. In the time of our ancestors, however, there was little expectation of such privacy.

At the National Archives, surviving records are in the MH series of records. These include the records of private madhouses from 1798 to 1812 in MH 51/735, records of pauper lunatics in MH12, some of which have been digitized, as well as some related records in MH 15, MH 17, MH 51 and MH 94. Records from County Lunatic Asylums are likely to be found in the relevant local county record offices.

A good starting-point for finding extant asylum records is The Hospital Records Database, a joint project of the Wellcome Library and the National Archives. Although it is no longer being updated, it has finding aids for hospital records, including asylum records and can be searched by hospital name or location. While many of the county records are searchable from the National Archives Discovery search page, some county record offices have more comprehensive catalogues on their individual web pages which can be found either through the National Archives 'Find an Archive' page or through a simple web search. For a comprehensive mental health history timeline and many scholarly articles, visit Andrew Robert's Study More website in association with the Middlesex University.

Ancestry holds the Lunacy Patients Admission Registers from 1846 to 1912 as well as the index to records of the St Lawrence Asylum in Bodmin, Cornwall from 1840 to 1900. Findmypast holds the Bexley, Kent Asylum Minute Books from 1901 to1939, the Prestwich Asylum Admissions from 1851 to 1901, and the South Yorkshire Asylum Admission Records along with Bethlem Hospital casebooks from 1683 to 1932. Check often for new additions.

Even though records for your ancestor may not survive, reading patient records and case books for others in your ancestors' time will give insight into the treatments and prevalent attitudes towards mental illness in the period.

MORTALITY

Nothing in life is quite as certain as death, but overall, our ancestors' life expectancy was considerably lower than ours today. Certainly, as we've already learned, there were extraordinarily high rates of infant and child mortality in the past, but even those ancestors who survived to adulthood were likely to die at a much younger age than if they had lived in our time. Whether due to war, famine, illness, accident, poor nutrition, poor sanitation and other contributing factors, many of our ancestors did not live to see their fiftieth birthdays and few attained the advanced ages we've come to expect in our generation.

Over time, life expectancy rose as medical advances, economic improvements and environmental controls improved the standards of life and the advances brought by the Industrial Revolution were particularly instrumental in improving overall mortality rates, especially amongst infants and children. In the mid-sixteenth century, rough estimates place the life expectancy of our ancestors at less than thirty-five years but by the mid-nineteenth century, life expectancy was about forty-five years and this number continued to grow at a relatively steady rate throughout the late nineteenth and early twentieth centuries, reaching just under seventy years by about 1950.

The statistics for life expectancy throughout history clearly show significant dips that resulted from both war and the occasional national scale epidemics of disease. At such times throughout history, some of our ancestors might have lost their lives prematurely as soldiers or as victims of widespread contagions such as the bubonic plague, cholera, smallpox and typhoid. As more detailed statistics became available throughout the nineteenth century, differences in the life expectancies of women and men became apparent, with women at risk from childbirth. At the same time, the life expectancy for those who lived in rural communities was noted to be considerably higher than residents of urban environments, with the attendant poverty, overcrowding and poor sanitary conditions that prevailed in many towns and cities during the industrial age.

Certainly, in the time of our ancestors, it was considered a newsworthy accomplishment for people to live to an advanced age and reports of octogenarians, nonagenarians and even centenarians can be found in the newspapers of the time, often expounding on their advice to others wishing to live to their advanced years. Lucky were those who reached this age in good health or who were in the care of their children since the only alternative for the elderly and infirm was generally the workhouse. In 1892, with Queen Victoria herself in her mid-seventies, a Royal Commission was convened to consider whether any alterations in Poor Law relief should be made in consideration of the increasing numbers of the poor and destitute elderly. Their findings were that no fundamental changes were required, and that it would be undesirable to interfere with the ability of the Poor Law guardians to deal with individual cases based on their merits. It would not be until 1908 that pensions for those over 70 would be introduced.

To what age did most of your ancestors live? Did the men live longer than the women? Was there a marked change in longevity over time? Recent research has suggested our propensity for longevity might be passed down to us from our ancestors in our DNA. Did one branch of your family generally outlive another and if so, what do you think were the contributing factors?

Case Study – Centenarian

A child born in 1770 England stood an almost 20 per cent chance of dying before their first birthday. For those who survived, their life expectancy was about forty or forty-five years although over 1 per cent of women would die earlier in childbirth. This case study looks at one woman who beat those odds, using genealogical records and newspaper articles from the time.

Shirley Morse Robinson was born on 11 April 1770 to parents Henry Robinson and Shirley Spencer in Welbeck Street near Cavendish Square and was baptized at the parish church of St Marylebone on 3 May 1770. When she was 18 years old, she married Philip Codd on 12 April 1788 at the Anglican Church in Oostende, West Vlaanderen, Belgium. Together, they had sixteen children, fourteen of whom grew to adulthood. Widowed at 60, Shirley enjoyed good health for most of her life.

By the time Shirley was 80, she had gone to live with her daughter Myra and her son-in-law Barclay Watson in Paddington. When she died on 17 January 1871 at the home of her son Edward, Shirley Morse Cobb was in her one hundred and first year. She had outlived her husband by forty years and all but two of her children. She was buried on 21 January 1871 at Stockbury Church near Sittingbourne, Kent.

Shirley Codd lived through the signing of the US Declaration of Independence, the French Revolution, the Battle of Waterloo and the abolition of slavery in the British Empire. She saw the first convicts transported to Australia and might have visited the Great Exhibition

---

in London. She would have experienced the Industrial Revolution and witnessed the first commercial steam engines, the first railways and the invention of the telegraph. When she was born, the Crown belonged to King George the III and through her life, she would have seen it pass to first King George the IV, then King William IV and finally to Queen Victoria.

Shirley Morse Cobb, centenarian, beat the odds.

Resources

Overall mortality statistics before the advent of civil registration in July 1837 are challenging to compile but many historians and statisticians have assembled and correlated available data and compiled estimations. One source is the weighty volume titled *The Population History of England 1541-1871*, a reconstruction by Wrigley and Schofield.

From the beginning of the nineteenth century, data is both more plentiful and more accurate. The published census reports for England, Wales, Scotland and Ireland between 1801 and 1937 along with the published registration reports from the General Register Office from 1837 to 1920 are available to search and browse on the Online Historical Population Reports website known as Histpop.

Since the end of the twentieth century with the merger of the Central Statistical Office and the Office of Population Censuses and Surveys, the Office for National Statistics has been charged with the collection and publication of statistics related to the United Kingdom. While most of the information on their website is more recent, they do sometimes publish information relevant to social history studies.

Newspapers are also good sources of information for mortality information. Use search terms such as 'mortality rolls' or 'age at death' to find relevant articles. To locate more unusual or newsworthy exceptions, search for terms such as 'centenarian', or 'four generations'.

Yet another valuable source of statistics is your own genealogy data. Many of the popular genealogy software programs can create statistical reports about your ancestors and some offer custom reports based on criteria you enter. Try reporting on different branches of your family to see if one ancestral line might have had greater longevity than another or create a report on the most common causes of death in your family.

DEATH AND BURIALS

Although hardly a cheerful topic, deaths and burials were familiar events to our ancestors and understanding their customs and views on the topic will bring you closer to understanding how they lived in their time. With high infant and child mortality rates, relatively short lifespans and epidemic diseases like smallpox and cholera, our ancestors no doubt attended many funerals, and were practised mourners at an early age.

Most of our ancestors from the time of the Reformation in the sixteenth century until the mid-nineteenth century would most likely have been laid to rest in the burial grounds of their parish church, in consecrated ground, unless circumstances, such as suicide, lunacy or murder prohibited such an action. Lunatics and those who committed suicide and were judged to have been in their right mind at the time (known as *felo de se*), would be buried at night, without any religious ceremony and outside the consecrated ground of the parish church cemetery. Many suicides, however, were exempted from this indignity if their suicide was judged as having happened during a period of temporary insanity (known as *non-compos mentis*).

By the nineteenth century, with the country's growing population, the historic parish burial grounds were becoming overcrowded and in many places, there was a growing concern about the unhealthy odours emanating from the vicinity of the graves. With the passing of the Burial Acts of 1857, cities with concerns about their overflowing burial grounds were permitted to buy new land outside of town and away from the churches. Such burial grounds were normally run as a business. A part would be consecrated while another part would be left unconsecrated for the use of dissenting religions and for burials not permitted in consecrated ground.

Having a 'proper' funeral was important to our ancestors and the possibility that they might suffer the ignominy of an anonymous burial prompted many of the nineteenth-century poor to join a burial club, the forerunner of today's life insurance. Their members paid a small weekly or monthly fee for a guaranteed payout on the death of the registered party, sufficient to provide a decent burial. In the early days of burial clubs, unscrupulous individuals registered the birth of a fictitious child, enrolled the child in a burial club, and then registered the death of the non-existent child to put in a claim. Later, when proof of death was required to obtain a death certificate, there were some horrific cases reported in the news of people who had committed murder for the sole purpose of collecting the burial club money.

The period of mourning for our ancestors was dictated by custom, with widows often remaining in mourning clothes for a full two years after the death of their husband. During the prescribed mourning period, women wore black clothing, often made of parramatta silk or bombazine with a matte finish, and greatly restricted their social activities. Men in deep mourning simply wore a black armband for the duration. Printed guides were published that dictated the proper mourning period depending on the closeness of the relationship to the deceased. During mourning, the only jewellery permitted was mourning jewellery often made from black enamel or jet. It was common for this mourning jewellery to include miniatures or photographs of the deceased, or a lock of their hair.

Our ancestors were both more accustomed to death and perhaps more morbidly fascinated, even obsessed, with the rituals and customs surrounding it. By viewing your genealogy data as a timeline, you will be able to figure out how many loved ones your ancestors buried and how many years of their lives they were likely to have spent in mourning dress.

Case Study – Baron Heath's Funeral

When Baron Heath, the Italian Consul in London, died in Paris at the age of 63 of congestion, it was a shock not only to his family, but to his home community of Croydon. His remains were transported back to England where preparations for a fitting send-off were already under way. This case study details the elaborate funeral mounted for the deceased, using genealogical records and newspaper articles from the time.

Baron Heath, the Italian Consul in London, and long-time resident of Croydon, departed this life at a quarter to eight on Monday morning, 5 June 1882, in Paris where he had been on a short holiday. Arrangements were at once to repatriate his remains. His corpse was secured in a packing crate and shipped by train from Paris to Dieppe where it was loaded aboard a vessel to cross the Channel to

Newhaven. The crate was then loaded into a van of the Brighton Railway Company for its final journey to Croydon. His coffin, made of polished oak with brass mountings and lined with lead sheeting, was met at the train station by the undertaker's hearse. Family and friends were in attendance and followed the funeral car in cabs.

The day of the funeral, Saturday, 10 June 1872, dawned unsettled and rainy, in observance of the mood of friends and family as they prepared to say their last farewells to the Baron who was to be buried in the quiet cemetery at Shirley parish. Many townspeople and estate employees gathered to pay their respects to the man who had done so much for the town and the neighbourhood.

As the elaborate funeral car bearing the coffin wound along the road, it was followed by the chief mourners walking and several carriages travelling in procession. The convoy rolled through the private grounds of Shirley Park before being joined at the church road by the Whitgift Cadet Corps and about seventy scholars of the Whitgift College.

At the church, the Shirley choir, accompanied by members of the Croydon Parish Church choir, sang hymns in solemn reverence and the Rev. W. Wilks read the service over the flower and wreath covered coffin. In deference to the deceased, the principal establishments around the town were partly closed with even the police court suspending proceedings during the funeral. The flags were flown at half-mast from the towers of the parish church and Whitgift College and in mid-afternoon a muffled peal was heard from the bells of the church.

A fine send-off indeed for a highly-esteemed man.

Resources

The standard genealogical records such as death certificates and burial records will give the names, dates, places and causes of death. Probate records will occasionally give clues to the wishes of the deceased for their burial arrangements. Take a close look at the burial place of your ancestor. Were they laid to rest in the burial grounds of the parish church or in one of the new city cemeteries? For church burials, often the only record will be found in the parish register, while for non-parochial burials more detailed records might exist so don't neglect contacting the cemetery office. Did your ancestor dictate their preference of burial manner or place in their will? Was their grave marker elaborate or simple in design? What was written on it and what can you infer from the inscription?

If you haven't seen your ancestor's burial place in person, check to see if a volunteer has photographed the headstone and posted it to one of the online burial websites such as Find a Grave. Contact the local county record office or family history society to see if memorial inscriptions have been recorded for the cemetery. Sometimes memorial inscriptions survive even where the grave marker does not.

Occasionally, the land that was the original burial place of an ancestor was later re-purposed for a different use. In this case, the graves were exhumed and the bodies and markers were relocated to another site. Research the history of the cemetery where your ancestor was buried.

Deaths, even more than births and marriages, were important events in our ancestors' lives and were often recorded in the newspapers, most commonly as a simple notice of death but sometimes as an obituary. For more prominent citizens, newspapers sometimes also included accounts of the funeral such as in the case study in this section.

Standards for mourning periods and customs were prescribed in popular publications in the Victorian period. Search digitized books and magazines for details of the acceptable conventions and rituals in your ancestors' time.

Chapter 5

WORK, WAGES AND ECONOMY

Early in the seventeenth century, the economy of Britain was primarily dependant on agriculture but that began to change with the colonization of the Americas and the West Indies. Not only did England's economy benefit from exporting goods to the colonists, but also from importing sugar and tobacco. At about the same time, trade with the East was established, primarily through the East India Company, which traded in bullion, textiles and tea. Eager to keep the benefits of this new global trade inside Britain's empire, Parliament enacted a series of Navigation Acts beginning in 1651, forbidding the colonies to trade except through British ships and British ports.

These trade restrictions, in combination with the duties and tariffs that England imposed on the colonies, set the stage for the American Revolution that raged from April 1775 until September 1783. The impact of this war on Britain's economy was immense. Not only was there the expense of supporting an army on the other side of the Atlantic, but the interruption of trade resulted in a recession and falling stock and land prices at the same time that taxes were raised to support the war effort.

By the end of the eighteenth century, the newly-independent United States and the West Indies were consuming more than half of British exports and supplied over 30 per cent of the imports of raw materials such as cotton. Throughout the nineteenth century, trade with the East also grew. The East India Company took control of India after expelling the Dutch, French and Portuguese and after the Opium Wars in the mid-nineteenth century, trade with China became more advantageous as the imports of tea and silk were offset with opium exports from India.

But back home in Britain, the beginning of the nineteenth century saw an escalation in hostilities with France and the outbreak of the Napoleonic Wars in 1803. The resulting increase in spending on military reinforcements again gave rise to high taxes and a marked rise in food

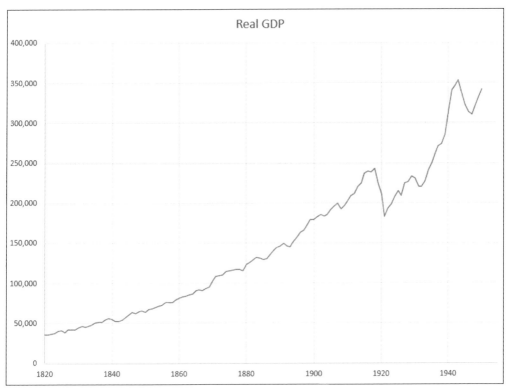

The economy improved throughout the nineteenth century: GDP 1820 to 1950.
(Graph based on data from Measuring Worth website)

prices while at the same time trade restrictions led to unemployment. These same trade restrictions also contributed to the United States once again declaring war on Britain and Ireland and British North America in June 1812. In December 1814, the Treaty of Ghent was signed, ending the war between the British and the United States and the defeat of Napoleon at Waterloo in June 1815 ended the Napoleonic Wars, leading to a period of relative peace.

Throughout the French Revolutionary Wars, a revolution of another kind was taking place in Britain. From about 1760, cottage industry manufacturing slowly gave way to new manufacturing processes that utilized mechanisation in factories driven by more efficient water power and eventually steam. The advances of this Industrial Revolution along with the end of the wars with France and America provided a major turning-point in Britain's economic history. Production and exports of textiles and metal goods were dramatically improved and a period of sustained economic growth followed, continuing into the twentieth century.

Through the research techniques and resources in this chapter, you will be able to juxtapose your ancestors' occupations and financial status against the backdrop of the economic realities of their time and place and have a greater understanding of their place in the socioeconomic history of their community.

ECONOMY

While Britain's economy was most assuredly affected by many factors including the influence of wars, revolutions and industrialization, our ancestors were most likely more concerned about the effects of these events on their own particular economic circumstances. By researching the various situations that contributed to rises and falls in the national economy, you can learn more about ebb and flow in the living standards of your ancestors in their time and place.

The standards by which our ancestors measured their level of economic security would have differed over time and by place and by family situation. To some of our ancestors, having adequate shelter, enough to eat and a suit of clothes to wear might have seemed out of reach while to others, the mounting costs and tax burdens of maintaining a large country estate might have threatened to change a lifestyle enjoyed for generations. Economic security or distress were relative to circumstance.

The idiom 'Keeping up with the Joneses' reminds us of a benchmark for socioeconomic worth. Measure your ancestor's wealth or status by comparing it to those of his neighbours, friends and co-workers. Was he poor in comparison to his contemporaries or did he count himself as more fortunate than most? Consider your ancestor's wealth in context with the average wages, cost of commodities and the prices of their time. While earnings of thirty shillings a week or an inheritance of a pound may seem like trivial amounts, when they are considered in the context of a loaf of bread costing less than tuppence, then they are much more impressive.

For those who are not familiar with the old British currency used before decimalization, amounts and calculations can sometimes be confusing. There were twenty shillings to the pound and twelve pence to the shilling. An amount of one pound, five shillings and sixpence

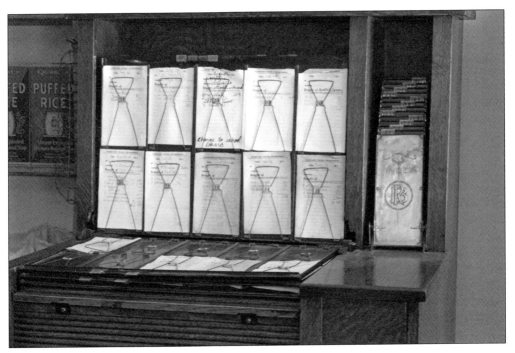

Running a tab at the local shops was common.

would be written as £1/5/6d while ten shillings might be written as 10/. A guinea was generally valued at about 21 shillings (£1/1s) and a crown was worth 5 shillings.

Case Study – Riot in Barrow-Upon-Soar 1795

In the following case study, we seek to understand the depth of desperation experienced by the poor in Britain after the bad harvests of 1794 combined with the demands of the army raised to fight France in 1795 on food resources. Details for the case study came primarily from historical newspapers where this riot and others like it around Britain were described in detail and seemingly with more compassion than judgement.

When France declared war on England on 1 February 1793, there was an immediate impact on Britain's economy. The United Kingdom was not prepared for the war, with many of their troops deployed around the world and the government hastily authorized an immediate increase of 25,000 soldiers. At the same time, the hot, dry summer of

---

1794 had resulted in a poor wheat harvest and this was followed by an extremely cold winter. By the spring of 1795, wheat was scarce and the prices of bread had risen dramatically. The large numbers of men who enlisted in the army and navy resulted in many families becoming dependant on the parish and the military's need for food resulted in yet greater shortages. Riots broke out in cities across Britain.

In Barrow-upon-Soar in Leicestershire on the evening of Wednesday, 5 August 1795, a wagon loaded with wheat passing through the town on its way to a baker in Leicester was stopped by a mob of hungry villagers and taken to the local church. The Mayor was notified, and he called upon a troop of cavalry from Leicester for aid. At the church, the people refused to give up the wheat, even after having been offered a part of it. For the previous several days, the bakers had no bread for sale, and the people of Barrow and the nearby villages of Sileby and Quorn were desperate.

The Riot Act was read to the assemblage and after more negotiations, it was finally agreed to release most of the wheat, conditional on the villagers being allowed to keep eight quarters of it. (A quarter of wheat is equivalent to eight bushels.) As the cavalry left with the wagonload of wheat, they were pelted with brickbats and fired upon, and were forced under the circumstances to return fire. William Oliver, Joseph Raven and John Mitchel were all killed instantly and another nine men were badly wounded, including William Roper who later died from the shot that shattered his leg.

From *Saunders's Newsletter* of 20 August 1795: 'John Mitchel, one of the killed, was an inhabitant of Sileby, and had been drawn to the fatal spot, partly by curiosity, partly by some unavoidable business; he has left behind him a wife and seven children, and the character of an unoffending harmless man: he was shot in the breast, fell backwards, and died without a groan.'

While accounts of the tragedy at Barrow-upon-Soar do not include information about the fate of Mitchel's widow and orphaned children, it is most likely that, without John Mitchel's income, they would have had little choice but to throw themselves on the charity of the parish.

Resources

Documents collected during genealogical research may show amounts of money paid or owed. Probate documents show bequests left to heirs. Land records often show how much a tenant paid a landlord for the privilege of occupying and farming their holding and tax records may show the annual taxes paid for various properties by the owner or occupier. These amounts, usually in pounds, shillings and pence, must be analysed according to their value relevant to the time and place.

An excellent resource for converting yesterday's sums of money into amounts relative today is the Measuring Worth website. The calculators on the website are quite unique in that they offer a variety of measures to do these conversions. The measures used are dependent on what type of transaction or asset is being converted and what indicator or adjustment seems most suited to the task.

Many historians and economists have studied the social history of the economy and a selection of informative articles by professional scholars can be found on the Victorian Web in the section on Economy. The subjects range from the general to the specific and new articles are added regularly. Similarly, search Google Scholar for articles on the history of the economy in the United Kingdom.

OCCUPATIONS

In England, the population enumerated during the 1841 census was just over 18.6 million people. Of these, less than 3 per cent said they were of independent means and less than 1 per cent were paupers, beggars or alms persons. Of the rest, 37 per cent gave an occupation of some kind while the rest were most likely their dependent families. So, with few exceptions, our ancestors spent most of their waking hours working at some occupation just to survive. Some worked on the land, planting crops such as rye or barley or raising livestock such as sheep or poultry. Some worked with their hands as blacksmiths or carpenters or masons. Some worked in the textile industry as weavers or spinners or as dressmakers or milliners or shoemakers making finished goods. Some were seamen or coachbuilders or horse trainers, while others were innkeepers, brewers or publicans. But however our ancestors earned their living, it is likely they worked from sunrise to sunset most days for wages that were just enough to pay the rent and put a meagre amount of food on the table.

The Industrial Revolution brought an end to local cottage industries.

Traditionally, many of our ancestors followed the occupation of their father, who in turn had followed the occupation of his father, with skills being handed down throughout the generations in an informal apprenticeship. Men would often be identified by their occupations such as George Brown the farmer or George Brown the tailor. Where a father had no skill to hand down, or where he had more sons than work, he might apprentice his son to the master of another trade in a nearby town for seven years, so the boy might learn a suitable trade. But as the industrial towns began to grow and expand and the demand for rural labour fell in the nineteenth century, many sons abandoned their family occupations and left their ancestral villages in seek of employment in the new mills and factories being built.

Some of the occupations they took up were dangerous. Hatters developed dementia from using mercury in the production of felt, giving rise to the expression 'mad as a hatter'. Chimney sweeps as young as 4 climbed down hot flues, sometimes getting stuck or suffocating or burning to death, and those who survived often developed cancer from the carcinogenic soot. File grinders and other metal workers who survived the flying metal and exploding grinding wheels would develop respiratory disease and seldom lived to their fortieth birthdays. The navvies who worked building railways and tunnels sometimes paid with their lives for the privilege and it was almost accepted that there might be a man lost for every mile of railway line built.

Besides simply knowing the occupations of our ancestors, to truly understand how they worked we also need to learn what their

England's working class in 1841.

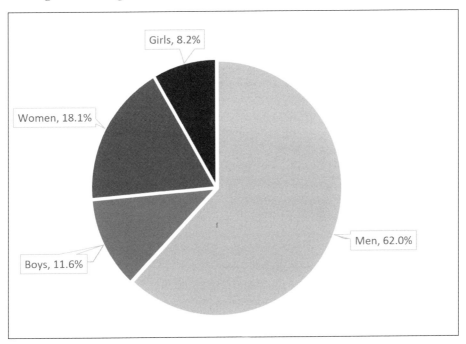

occupation entailed. What hours did they work? What challenges did they face? What conditions did they work in? You must figuratively roll up your sleeves and work beside them, driving the plough, stoking the blast furnace or boiling the hops and making the beer if you want to learn their stories.

Case Study – Framework Knitters

The following case study explores the devastating economic effects of the Industrial Revolution on the cottage industry of framework knitting in rural Leicestershire. Details for the case study came primarily from historical newspapers, census records and the Framework Knitters Museum website.

By the mid-nineteenth century, the men of Dadlington in Leicestershire were for the most part framework knitters, although the occasional man still farmed the land. For those who did piecework, knitting mostly coarse cotton hose or the infrequent lacy shawl on the large and noisy machines, life was difficult indeed. They earned, on average, about 5s 3d a week and sometimes that was a struggle. Often their wives and children were also put to work, and a family who worked hard together might earn as much as 7s 9d.

But that wage would seldom last the week. The rent of their house would take a precious 1s and coals to warm their hands to work another 10d. Candles to light their work area after sunset, another 9d. Meagre food to feed the family would claim the rest. Rice 4d, Salt ½d, Milk 3-½d, Bacon 7d, Bread 2s, 2-½d, Sugar 3-½d, Potatoes 1s 5-½d. By the end of the week, the food gone and the children hungry, many would be forced to take their Sunday clothes to the pawnbroker just to survive, hoping that, by the following weekend they could earn enough to buy them back so they could look respectable at church.

Such was the case of John Hammond and his wife Catherine in June 1839. Unable to pay the poor rate of the parish which amounted to 2s 2d on his humble earnings, Hammond was handcuffed by the constable and dragged from his wife and six small children to gaol where he would remain for thirteen weeks. His wife and children,

---

thus left without support, were evicted from their home and forced to enter the Bosworth Workhouse.

A Royal Commission was convened to enquire into the conditions of framework knitters in 1845, on receipt of a petition signed by 25,000 people. The Commission produced three volumes with the first containing its report and the other two containing the minutes of the evidence, but it was a case of 'too little, too late' for the families of Dadlington.

By the 1860s, only four framework knitting families remained in Dadlington. Most of the stocking work had long since moved to the factories where large operations and inexpensive labour had driven down the cost of hose. By the 1870s only two framework knitters remained in Dadlington and by the 1880s, there were none. The men of the village had returned to their farming roots.

Framework knitting machine.

Resources

The occupations of our ancestors can be found on many traditional genealogical records including, but not limited to, apprenticeship documents, census records, parish records, civil birth, marriage and death records, wills and probate documents, burial records, deeds and tax records. As you locate these various documents, you may discover your ancestor worked in the same occupation their entire life or you may find career changes, particularly during the industrial revolution. Look for historical directories that might list your ancestors' occupation or business. A great source for these is the Special Collections archive held by the University of Leicester.

For the more obscure occupations that are found on records, many lists have been published online and a definition for an archaic term can usually be found with a simple internet search. For example, a search shows the term 'boardwright' was used to describe a carpenter and 'inspectors of nuisances' were the sanitary inspectors or environmental health officers of long ago.

1841 Services Sector.

A good resource for statistical information about occupations are the reports created from the data of the decennial censuses of England, Wales and Scotland. The website A Vision of Britain Through Time has many reports and maps as well as a statistical atlas which shows the dispersal of various occupations throughout Britain at various times. Also useful are the various statistical reports published by the government after the census data was collated which can be found by searching digital historical book archives with a search term 'Census statistics' followed by your place of interest.

To learn the fundamentals of your ancestors' occupation, search for digitized books contemporary to your ancestors' time and place in the online libraries listed in the first chapter. As examples, Abercrombie and

The 1841 census provided the first real view of the distribution of occupations.

1841 Agricultural Sector.

1841 Construction Sector.

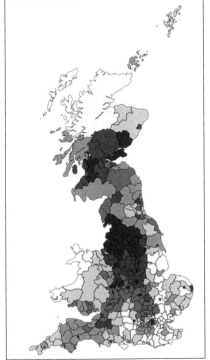

1841 Manufacturing Sector.

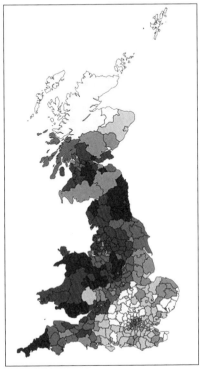

1841 Mining Sector.

Mawe published a book for gardeners in 1787 called *Every Man His Own Gardener* and Bradley published a book about coaching in 1889 called *Old Coaching Days in Yorkshire*. Similarly, search journals and periodicals contemporary to your time period for fascinating occupational insights such as can be found in Stott's article 'On the Mortality among Innkeepers, Publicans, and other Persons engaged in the Sale of Intoxicating Liquors' published in 1876 in the *Journal of the Institute of Actuaries and Assurance Magazine*, digitized on jStor.

BUSINESSES AND EMPLOYERS

Our early ancestors most likely worked on the land, provided services to the gentry or manufactured goods in small-scale cottage industries. But as the Industrial Revolution began to change the very fabric of life in Britain during the late eighteenth and early nineteenth centuries, the development of steam power and mechanization gave birth to countless new businesses and manufactories. With the recent innovations in agriculture, more food could be produced with less manual labour, creating a surplus of agricultural labourers and severe unemployment in rural areas. The cottage industries that had sustained spinners, weavers and other small manufacturers for centuries were suddenly unable to compete with the prices and quality of goods produced by mechanical means. People began to leave the countryside to find work in towns and cities and those who would have previously worked for themselves became dependent on an employer for their livelihood.

As you learned in the last section, many genealogical records state the occupation of our ancestors. Such sources might include church parish records, land and taxation records, census records, probate documents, civil registration certificates or census records, to name but a few. But while these records might list an occupation, it is rare that they also list the employer or the name of the business where our ancestor was employed. Usually, it is only by researching your ancestors' occupations in depth and the businesses that operated in the area in which they lived that you can sometimes figure out their employers and thereby enrich your family story with added historical context.

Case Study: Barrow Ship Building Company

The following case study examines the early history of the Barrow Ship Building Company and the lives of five young men who worked there in various capacities. In 1881, Henry Welch, John Clucas, Thomas Walker, Robert Hamilton and Patrick Keenan were all recently arrived in Barrow-in-Furness, an up-and-coming shipbuilding centre in Lancashire (now Cumbria). Details for the case study came primarily from historical newspapers, census records and Grace's Guide, an online source of information about industry and manufacturing in Britain during the industrial revolution period.

In the 1830s, Barrow-in-Furness, Lancashire was just a hamlet in the small parish of Dalton-in-Furness, the whole of which was home to less than 3,000 parishioners. Although small quantities of ore were produced there, it wasn't until Henry Schneider, an iron speculator, discovered large deposits of haematite iron ore in the middle of the century that Barrow's potential as an industrial town was seen. Schneider founded the Furness Railway to transport the ore, setting the stage for further development.

By 1871, Barrow's population had swelled to over 18,000 people with an influx of workers from the surrounding rural communities but also from as far away as Scotland and Ireland who came in search of employment in the growing shipbuilding works. It was in mid-February 1871, that three new companies were formed in Barrow-in-Furness. The largest, the Eastern Steamship Company, with capital of £500,000, would trade between Barrow-in-Furness and India and China to the east through the newly opened Suez Canal. Supplying Eastern Steamship with ships would be the Barrow Ship Building Company, formed with a working capital of £100,000. The third firm, Barrow Rolling Mills Company, held a further £100,000 of capital and would employ the ironmasters, iron founders and engineers needed to manufacture and sell the rails, bars, plates, tin plates, fittings and machinery for the ships. All three of the new companies benefitted from the backing of many wealthy and influential investors, most notably William Cavendish, the Duke of Devonshire, who invested heavily in all three enterprises, and James Ramsden who had been the mayor of Barrow-in-Furness since 1867 and who was destined to be knighted the following year.

Over the next decade, the population of Barrow had predictably more than doubled with about 47,000 people now calling the seaside town home. In 1881, one of the town's new residents was Henry Welch, a single, 24-year-old foreman plater living in the Ramsden Dock Cottages. John Clucas, also 24 years old, was originally from the Isle of Man and he worked as a shipyard labourer. Clucas, along with a handful of other young men from the Isle of Man, boarded with the widow Eleanor Cannell on Hall Street. Thomas Walker, aged 15, lived with his family on Bath Street. The Walker family had arrived in Barrow less than a decade previously from Staffordshire and Thomas' father William was a fireman at the steelworks while his 12-year-old brother George worked in Barrow's jute factory. The Hamilton family too had moved to Barrow from Scotland at about the same time as the Walkers. Robert Hamilton, aged 33, was a ship's carpenter, and he lived with his wife Mary and their two small children at the Devonshire Buildings. Patrick Keenan, aged 40, was born in Ireland but had met and married his wife Nasan in Scotland. The Keenans had six children in their household, the youngest of whom was only 2 years old.

Like so many young men in the latter part of the nineteenth century, these sons, fathers or husbands had journeyed, either alone or with their families, far from their ancestral homes to a rapidly growing industrial town. They were eager for gainful employment and were determined to prosper in the fledgling ship building works they found in Barrow-in-Furness. Although these five men had little in common, other than being recent arrivals in the post-industrial town and all being employees of the Barrow Ship Building Company, they would soon be linked together by a horrific and unimaginable disaster.

At about 11:30 am on 21 June 1881, as the Inman steamer, the *City of Rome*, was being launched from the Barrow Ship Building Company works, one of the two tubular boilers that powered the windlass and the anchor exploded and was hurled across the shipyard, travelling 500 feet before it buried itself in the sand. Nearly 50,000 spectators watched in horror as young Henry Welch was hurled sixty feet in the air, dying at once. John Clucas, the native of the Isle of Man who had been standing next to the boiler, suffered severe lacerations of his head and body and was rushed to the North Lonsdale Hospital but died soon after arrival. Thomas Walker, the young man from Staffordshire, was also cut badly and both of his legs were broken. He too died shortly after the accident. Robert Hamilton, the young father from Scotland, received serious injuries and was not expected to survive. Indeed, he died just after midnight, leaving behind a widow and two young children. Patrick Keenan, the Irishman with six children, was also severely wounded. He held on until 23 September when he finally succumbed to his injuries and was laid to rest in the Barrow Cemetery.

At the Coroner's inquest, it was determined the pressure in the boiler that Clucas oversaw had exceeded the recommended level of 38lbs, indeed had climbed as high as 70lbs, before exploding on deck and that the explosion was a direct result of Clucas' negligence in not keeping the steam down. Thomas Wood, the supervisor who was responsible for the safe operation of the boilers, testified Clucas was a 'very steady man and a teetotaller and had sufficient experience to qualify him', but his words made little difference to the Coroner and jury. Their final verdict was: 'We come to the conclusion that the poor men lost their lives through the explosion which was caused by an over-pressure of steam, and we suggest that the shipyard people should test their boilers periodically.' No blame was assigned to the Barrow Ship Building Company although it was agreed by all involved that it was a lamentable accident.

Resources

One of the best resources for information about businesses in the industrial age are historical city directories. The University of Leicester hosts a very comprehensive collection of digitized directories and others can be found on Google Books, the Internet Archive or on the shelves in local libraries and archive offices.

For detailed information about the companies operating in your ancestors' town or city, study historical newspapers and periodicals. Although local papers are most likely to mention local businesses, don't discount finding pertinent articles in larger publications throughout the UK. You can expect to find articles related to almost every aspect of businesses, from the formation of new companies and the failure of others to details of investors, dividends, new sales or projects, labour union actions as well as mention of businesses in current news stories or social news. It is even possible to find your ancestor mentioned by name in association with his or her employer.

Most business records, where they survive, are held by local archives and these may contain information about the dates of operation or possibly annual reports, accounts and correspondence. The National Archives at Kew holds the Companies' Registration Office records in BT31 and BT41, but these do not include records of the businesses themselves, only the registration and dissolution of companies between 1844 and 1980. Search the Discovery catalogue on the National Archives website to find records from over 2,500 archives across the UK or do an internet search for archives in your area of interest. Larger corporations still in operation may have elected to keep their own archives, so it is well worth doing a general web search. A wonderful example of a self-hosted archive is the collection of materials held in the Thomas Cook Company Archives with photographs and travellers' diaries and other company materials dating from present day back to the founder's first excursion in 1841.

Once you have identified the business your ancestor likely worked for, research its owners, its inception and, if applicable, its demise. Check newspapers and periodicals to find out if the business was involved in any labour disputes, controversies or industrial accidents. What role did it play in the community and how did it contribute to the growth or the decay of the town or city it was part of? What were the working hours for the business? How was your ancestors' working day affected by the various Factory Acts introduced the nineteenth century? Did the employees work from dawn to dusk six days a week as was often the case in the early industrial period? Was your ancestor employed there for his entire working life or was it just a stepping stone in his career? Can you find any images of the workplace or descriptions of the business in newspapers, periodicals or trade journals?

Each new morsel of information can add perspective to your ancestors' working life and bring you closer to knowing who they were and how they spent their days.

SOCIAL WELFARE AND RELIEF

One of the earliest efforts to control the poor in England began in 1495 when Parliament passed the Vagabonds and Beggars Act, which stated that vagrants be placed in the stocks for three days and three nights on bread and water and then be sent out of town. By 1531, it was recognized not all the poor were responsible for their own condition and a new Act was passed, allowing the aged and impotent poor to apply for a licence to beg for alms while those who were capable of working were punished by whipping or being placed in the pillory.

The fate of the impotent poor took a turn for the worse shortly after this when the Reformation under Thomas Cromwell dissolved the monasteries between 1535 and 1540 and the benevolence of the nuns and monks disappeared. Recognizing this, a series of laws were passed throughout the late 1500s, attempting to care for the poor who were considered poor through no fault of their own with the parish giving a weekly allowance for their care, while those who were considered 'professional beggars' continued to be punished in the stocks, by whipping or by branding with a 'V'.

In 1601, the Elizabethan Act for the Relief of the Poor was the beginning of what many consider the period of the Old Poor Law. The act made parishes responsible for looking after their own poor. A compulsory poor rate tax was levied against the landowners of the parish and an overseer of the poor was appointed for each parish to collect the tax and dispense either food or money to the impotent poor and to put the able-bodied poor to work. No administrative standards were introduced, however, and the interpretation of the Act was left to the individual parish, leading to differences in the enactment of the law with some parishes being very lax with the poor and others taking their responsibilities to the extreme. Inevitably, this led to the idle poor seeking alms wherever they were most plentiful.

The Poor Relief Act of 1662, or the Settlement and Removals Act as it became known, established that each person belonged to the parish in which they were born, or in which they had established residency by meeting one of a series of conditions. The Act further stated that if a pauper became chargeable to a parish that was not his own, he could be ordered to return to his parish of settlement. Conditions of settlement included being born in a parish, having lived there for forty consecutive days without complaint, being employed in the parish for a year and a day or having an apprenticeship with a settled master, holding office or renting a property worth £10 per annum or by having married into the parish.

Further legislation, 'For Amending the Laws relating to the Settlement, Imployment and Relief of the Poor', enacted on 25 March 1723, called for the keeping of records of the poor. Under this act, each person who received or might receive assistance from the parish should be registered in a parish relief book after taking an oath stating a reasonable cause for seeking aid. The aid given should last no longer than the cause continued. The Act further granted the right for church wardens and overseers of the poor to buy or build poorhouses to lodge and employ the poor. Any pauper who refused to live in such a poorhouse would not be entitled to relief from the parish. Parishes too small to afford their own poorhouse were allowed to united with other parishes to establish a shared poorhouse.

By 1783, while it was recognized that the 'sufferings and distresses' of the poor were 'very grievous', the Act for the Better Relief and Employment of the Poor found the money raised for poor relief was often mismanaged, misapplied and often wasted in litigations about settlement rights. Under the Act, the overseers were no longer authorized to hire out the labour of the parish paupers under contract and all such existing contracts were to be terminated on 25 March 1783. Furthermore, while officials were still authorized to make contracts for the provision of food or clothing for the workhouse, these contracts were not to exceed twelve months, in an attempt to limit abuse of the system. All guardians of the poor were to be nominated at a public meeting where their salaries were also to be fixed. The Act also ordered more oversight in the administration of the poorhouse including regular reviews of the accounts. And while the Act provided for the impotent poor, the elderly, the infirm and the children, it gave authority to the overseers to put any able-bodied poor to work for their support and if work was refused, the overseers were authorized to send the offender to a House of Correction for a period of between three months and a year.

In 1832, recognising the inconsistencies, abuses and mismanagement of the poor throughout England, a Royal Commission was formed to do a full and complete study of poverty in the parishes. Their initial reports were issued in February 1833 and eventually their work filled thirteen volumes and recommended a radical change to the Poor Laws.

Women at mealtime at St Pancras Workhouse. (Via Peter Higginbottom).

Their report began:

> It is now our painful duty to report that in the greater part of the districts which we have been able to examine, the fund, which the 43rd of Elizabeth directed to be employed in setting to work children and persons capable of labour, but using no daily trade, and in the necessary relief of the impotent, is applied to purposes opposed to the letter, and still more to the spirit of that law, and destructive to the morals of the most numerous class, and to the welfare of all.

As a result of the Commission's findings, the 1834 Poor Law Amendment Act was passed, ending all out relief for the able-bodied and ensuring that, except under exceptional circumstances, the poor could only get help if they were prepared to leave their homes and enter the workhouse. To discourage idleness, workhouse conditions were deliberately harsh. Families would be split up. Paupers wore a uniform, and the food provided was meant to be just adequate to their needs but repetitious and uninteresting. Inmates were expected to work at menial tasks and children could expect to be hired out to work.

To organize aid to the poor, the parishes in England, then numbering about 15,000, were grouped into Poor Law Unions and each of the new unions was to have its own workhouse. Ireland did the same four years later in 1838, while Scotland set up a slightly different system in 1845, giving no relief to the able-bodied while still providing out relief to the impotent poor.

Unless they were financially well off, many of our ancestors might have had occasion at some point in their lives to receive assistance from the parish. Between the years of 1851 and 1860, the average population of the UK was 28,104,000 and the average number of paupers living in workhouses during the same period was 1,109,275 or 3.9 per cent. Were your ancestors among those who were down on their luck? Were they forced through circumstance to seek parochial relief? If they entered the workhouse, what were conditions like for them? Or perhaps they received out relief, a small allowance to help them get back on their feet again after an illness or death in the family. What events drove them to desperation and did they eventually recover from the setbacks they faced or did they become stuck in the endless cycle of poverty?

Case Study – The Cycle of Poverty

For some, relief was to be avoided at all costs, even if it meant going without. For others, relief from the parish was a lifestyle, one inherited from their parents. They were either on relief, in the workhouse or applying for relief throughout their lives, and made no great effort to earn a living in any other way. Such was the case of Mary Ann Ralph. At the age of 40, she was a widow, living in the Poplar Workhouse. Her three oldest children were in the charge of the Sutton Schools and the youngest, an illegitimate child only 2 years old, was in the Sick Asylum. Records used in this study include the Bromley Workhouse casebooks from the Booth Collection website, parish records, census records and workhouse admission and discharge records.

Mary Ann Price, the daughter of Charles and Mary Ann Price senior, married Thomas Ralph on 25 July 1869 at St. Philip's Church in Stepney. Thomas Ralph, described by Mary Ann's mother as 'being from a bad family', was a dock labourer and even after their marriage, Mary Ann sometimes worked as a hawker. By 1881, they were living at 11 Salmon Street in Stepney with two daughters, Mary Emily who was 5 years old and Eliza Jane who was 2 years old. Neighbours agreed it was likely that Mary Ann drove her husband Thomas to drink by her neglect and her own habit of drinking. Perhaps as a result of too much alcohol, Thomas died at the age of 36 on 22 May 1882, leaving two small daughters and Mary Ann pregnant with a third daughter who would be called Annie.

Mary Ann's father, Charles Price, had died that same spring and her mother was in and out of the workhouse. Her brother James was a bad character and had spent time in prison for stealing. James was a lighterman by trade and often neglected his own wife and children who had been forced to seek assistance from the parish several times. Her sister Jane's husband had just been discharged from the Sick Asylum, but while he'd been away, she had been to prison for stealing and had since moved in with another man. Although Mary Ann's brother Edward had been helping his mother and sisters by giving them £1 per week, he told the Relieving Officer that it all went to drink and he had reduced this to 10s and now only 5s a week rather than continue throwing good money away.

By July of 1883, Mary Ann Ralph told the Relieving Officer she had no means to keep her children and asked that they be admitted to the Workhouse Schools. Mary and Eliza were admitted and young Annie went to Mary Ann's sister Jane. No longer responsible for her children, Mary Ann decided she would go into service and obtained a situation at £16 per year but was soon let go. She quickly found a similar situation, but just as quickly was let go again. By February 1885, Mary Ann was staying with her mother and again requested and received medical assistance. Finally finding another situation, Mary Ann was again dismissed, having stolen and pawned articles belonging to her employer. Unsurprisingly, Mary Ann had spent the money on drink. She was sentenced to two months' hard labour for her actions and accordingly, on 16 December 1885, her sister Jane applied for Mary Ann's youngest child Annie to be admitted to the workhouse and the assistance was granted. On 29 July 1886, Mary Ann applied yet again for medical assistance and admission to the Sick Asylum, remaining there until she was discharged at her own request on 6 October.

In the later part of 1886, Mary Ann went to work for a Mr Tucker but by the first of the year in 1887, Tucker let the Relieving Officer know Mrs Ralph had left his employ after stealing his things and pawning them for money for drink. Mary Ann was once again sent to prison for a month of hard labour and after being released, she applied for admission to the workhouse, heavy with child. When the baby was born, she named it James and when asked for the father's name, she accused her former employer, Mr Tucker of seducing her. Tucker admitted paternity and although he paid 5s a week for the baby's care, the Ralph family remained in the care of the parish.

In and out of the schools; in and out of the sick asylum; in and out of the workhouse; in and out of jobs. Mary Ann Price and her children, like her parents before her, were stuck in a cycle of poor health, drunkenness, immorality and poverty.

Resources

With over 2,800 web pages dedicated to the institutions of the poor, Peter Higginbotham's website, The Workhouse, is an important online resource to learn more about poor laws, life in the workhouse and the historic details of workhouses where your ancestors may have stayed. Also an author, Higginbotham has written a number of books on various aspects of workhouse life that provide glimpses into the conditions our pauper ancestors might have encountered. Among his works are *The Workhouse Encyclopedia*, a fully-illustrated guide to every aspect of the workhouse, and *Life in A Victorian Workhouse*, focusing on the Victorian period.

Another excellent online resource for learning about the lives of the poor is the Charles Booth Online Archive. From 1886 to 1903, Charles Booth completed a survey of life and labour in London. As well as providing browsable and searchable maps of the poorest areas of the city, the website has digitized copies of Charles Booth's survey notebooks, police notebooks, Stepney Union casebooks and Jewish notebooks. Similarly, the London Lives website has searchable manuscripts dating between 1690 and 1800 that detail the crime, poverty and social policy in the metropolis of London.

Both Ancestry and Findmypast have searchable record sets ranging from workhouse records of admissions and discharges, school registers and infirmary registers and an increasing number of similar records are being made available on Family Search. Links to other valuable online resources can be found at the UK GDL link website or at Cyndi's List website.

Records related to workhouses and assistance to the poor not online can often be found in the local county record offices. Parish church records such as vestry minutes may include details of illegitimate children, settlement examinations of people who came to the parish or left it along with lists of apprenticeships arranged and the relief given to paupers, the sick and the elderly. Search the Discovery catalogue at the National Archives website to find the location of records in your area of interest or visit the websites of the individual county record offices to find out how to access their catalogue.

Google Books, Internet Archive and other similar websites have digitized publications of the Poor Law acts as well studies related to paupers and workhouses from the nineteenth century and there are many articles in newspapers contemporary to the time both on the changing laws governing the workhouses and even about individual paupers throughout Britain.

Chapter 6

COMMUNITY, RELIGION AND GOVERNMENT

Imagine your ancestor's life as the centre of three overlapping circles representing their community, their religion and their government. Each of these circles has overlaps with the other and at the convergence is your ancestor's life. Ripples of inevitable change through one of the circles would be felt in the others, affecting not only your ancestors but the lives of those around them, influencing the paths your ancestor followed and the decisions they made. This chapter will look at these circles and how they influenced our ancestors in their time and place.

Without the foundation of their community, our ancestors would have borne all the challenges life threw their way on their own shoulders. And without the needs of their community, they would have lived very isolated and singular lives. Instead, they joined clubs and

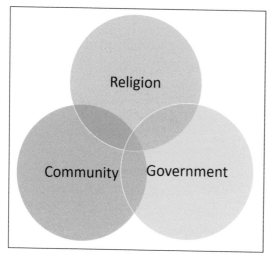

Community, religion and government convergence.

associations to support others in their neighbourhood and, at other times, looked to organizations of their fellow townspeople for assistance and encouragement. They attended local events such as fairs and markets and they celebrated holidays with the people around them.

Our ancestors were great joiners. They formed clubs and associations consistent with their beliefs, politics, activities, leisure pursuits and occupational interests, and affiliated themselves with others who shared their interests. In early history, tradesmen and businessmen of a town or city formed guilds for their occupations, not only to control the trade, but so that members could socialize and support each other. By the nineteenth century there were clubs for everything from agriculture to engineering to football. It is quite likely your ancestor belonged to at least one of them.

Before the eighteenth century, information and news of the day primarily spread throughout the community from person to person, mouth to mouth, no doubt most often at the local pub. With schools for the most part by tuition only, it was almost guaranteed that literacy and education were only for the well-to-do. Many of our ancestors would have inked their signatures by making their mark, unable to write even their own names. Books, newspapers and other reading materials were limited, both because of early printing challenges and because there was a general lack of audience with such a large percentage of the population illiterate.

Early modern English was sometimes casual and prone to localized dialects, riddled with slang and colloquial expressions. It was not until the mid-eighteenth century when Samuel Johnson published *A Dictionary of the English Language* that there were even set spelling conventions for words. Over time, those speaking the lower-class dialects were stigmatized and the colourful idioms and speech patterns fell out of use as people strove to speak correctly, removing the words from their vocabulary that marked them as unrefined.

From the eighteenth century and through the nineteenth, demand for printed materials increased with the expansion of industrialized trade and the growing wealth of middle-class people who earned their money rather than being born to it. While the falling price of newsprint and improved printing processes certainly paved the way for greater distribution of the printed word, it was when taxes were finally removed from newspapers that literature exploded for our ancestors.

The development of industry and agriculture and the formation of trade unions also created a demand for collected works of sorts although these were frequently of the radical or sensational genres. Mandatory schooling from 1870 along with an improved economy meant that more of our ancestors growing up at that time would learn to read before they were put to work out of necessity. As the only literate members of the household, they would be asked to read out loud to their families and pressed into service whenever there was a need for the written word.

From time immemorial, religion guided and influenced our ancestors' lives. There were few religious controversies of great significance until the reign of King Henry VIII. When faced with a wife unable to give him a son and a Pope who would not grant an annulment, King Henry turned his back on Rome and established the Church of England in 1534, all the while still defending his realm against the Lutherans.

One hundred years later, a series of conflicts took place in what has become known as the English Civil War. Between 1642 and 1646 and then again between 1648 and 1649, war rocked Britain as the Parliamentarians and Royalists fought over the manner of government. In the end, Charles I was tried and executed and his son, Charles II, was exiled. The monarchy was replaced by the Commonwealth of England which was in turn replaced by the Protectorate, with Oliver Cromwell at its head. It was not until after Cromwell's death that Charles II returned from exile and was restored to the throne in 1660.

During this same period in the sixteenth and early seventeenth century, we see clearly the effects of faith and religious persecution. No doubt the religious strife was nothing new, but it was during this period that religious dissenters, objecting to state interference in religious matters, separated themselves from the Established Church. Many Puritans, with growing disdain for the Church of England, left England's shores for the New World to take their chances amongst the natives in return for their religious freedom. The Quaker religion formed in the mid-seventeenth century. As a group, they refused to swear oaths or participate in wars. As their movement gained a significant following, they were at first persecuted along with other religious dissenters such as the Baptists and Congregationalists but finally in 1689, the Act of Toleration was passed, allowing freedom of worship to these Nonconformists, so long as they swore to the oaths of Allegiance and Supremacy and rejected transubstantiation.

This Act of Toleration did not, however, apply to Catholics. After the various Jacobite rebellions, the Catholic religion was driven underground, its practitioners taxed and fined as dissenters as well as being prohibited from taking office or assuming any official role. It was not until the early nineteenth century that the Roman Catholic Relief Act was passed and Catholics were emancipated in Britain.

Even during all the internal turmoil of civil war, dissenting religions and political coups, Britain continued to form alliances with other countries and to be involved in wars and conflicts abroad, all the while battling to keep control of the various colonies throughout her dominion. In the sixteenth and seventeenth centuries, Spain was a dominant player in the world and England often allied with France to battle against the Spanish. When Spain's power began to decline, however, the alliance between France and England disintegrated and by the eighteenth century, the two countries engaged in intermittent wars, struggling for control in Europe, or at least to prevent one another from taking control. At the same time, a race to control the Americas began amongst the European powers and control shifted from one to the other.

When the American War of Independence began in 1775, the French, seeing an opportunity, began to support the Americans, supplying their armies and providing intelligence to the rebels. The war ended in an American victory in 1783. The French support of the Americans came at a price, however, and the debts they incurred led to a financial crisis that sparked the French Revolution in the late eighteenth century. The revolution led to the execution of King Louis XVI in 1793 and in the aftermath, France declared war on Britain beginning the French Revolutionary Wars which were followed by the Napoleonic Wars.

While all of these religious and political conflicts belong to the subject of History with a capital H, as social historians and genealogists, our interest is in the effect that these events had on our ancestors' lives. Like ripples in a pond, the waves emanating from the larger events in our ancestors' time and place touched their lives and shaped their existence.

COMMUNITY

From time immemorial, our ancestors associated themselves with others, either informally or sometimes formally. The early clubs often met in the taverns, dining, drinking and socialising with one another. By the eighteenth century, with the introduction of coffee-drinking, clubs became a little more formal, and our ancestors met in the coffee houses of the day to discuss politics and religion, with many of these establishments becoming hotbeds of political scheming, posturing and intrigue.

The Freemasons were an ancient fraternity of operating masons active very early in England's history although by the early eighteenth century, they had expanded to allow non-masons into their circles. Another active membership organization in the eighteenth century, the Royal Foresters initiated members by combat with quarterstaffs, swords or cudgels. That ceased in 1843, not long after its members formed a Friendly Society, one of the forerunners of today's insurance companies. With origins as old, or older, the Oddfellows were a similar association who, besides meeting for social reasons, supported local charities. It was common throughout the eighteenth and nineteenth centuries for these groups to take part in any municipal gatherings with parades and bands, and for them to donate money to aid those in the direst need.

In the mid-nineteenth century, sporting clubs became popular. One of the oldest football clubs still in existence is the Dublin University Football Club, founded in 1854 at Trinity College, Dublin, Ireland although many other clubs no longer active were established considerably earlier, back to the sixteenth century. Besides football, our ancestors joined golf clubs in the eighteenth century. Cricket players formed teams to play for their towns and villages. Another sport, polo, was popular with British officers stationed in India and they brought it home to Britain in the mid-nineteenth century.

During the Victorian era, many associations were formed to pursue knowledge in the industrial age. Although farming is seldom mentioned in discussions of the effects of industrialization, for certain, advancements in the way farmers worked the land came fast and furious, even as the factories of the age were being built. The Royal Agricultural Society of England was founded as the English Agricultural Society in 1838, and its motto was 'Practice with Science'.

Women's groups were more likely to be informal, a casual gathering

The author's father, John Daniel Bond, Governor General's Horse Band.

of women with something in common, and often the women combined their philanthropic efforts in support of charitable causes. At the end of the nineteenth century, many women's groups took up the cry of the suffragettes, finding a collective political voice and urged the government to give women the vote.

Beyond those mentioned, there were hundreds if not thousands of clubs and associations in our ancestors' time. What was your ancestor a member of? What sorts of activities did they participate in? What other groups in the community supported your ancestors by fighting for their rights or by extending aid?

Case Study – The Spinning School

The Spinning School was a charitable school for girls established in York in 1782 for the girls of poor families by two benevolent ladies, Mrs Cappe and Mrs Gray. Many of the poor girls of the city in that time owe their survival to those two ladies. This case study looks at the founding of the school through an account written by Catharine Cappe in 1805.

The idea of the spinning school was first conceived when Mrs Cappe and Mrs Gray became concerned about the racy behaviour of the girls employed in a hemp factory in their local neighbourhood towards the end of 1782. Initially, the two women determined that they would teach the girls to read, knit and sew in the evenings, after they had finished work in the factory and that they would go with the group of girls to church services on Sundays. Soliciting donations totalling £11, 5s, 6d from their friends and acquaintances, they hired a woman to teach the girls.

Finding that the girls' characters were still in a perilous situation resulting from spending their days in the factory, they instead decided to set up a spinning school with the intent that the girls would leave the factory, and earn a comparable wage at the new school. The parents of the eighteen girls were approached with the proposition, and once they learned the girls would still receive the same wages, they gave their daughters over to the protection of the two women.

By July of 1785, the spinning school was established and shortly afterwards, a knitting school was formed. Through donations and

154

subscriptions, Mrs Gray and Mrs Cappe were able to offer what they considered the minimum suitable clothing to the girls in their charge and additional items could be earned by the girls if they increased the number of hanks of worsted they spun in a day. Those who managed six hanks were given a checked apron in addition to their regular two blue ones. With seven hanks, they received a cap, a coloured shawl and a pair of pattens which were protective overshoes to be worn over the second-hand shoes given to all the girls.

Rather than beating the girls to discipline them as their parents had done, girls found guilty of slacking when spinning would have their gown turned and worn inside out, or have a hank of worsted pinned to their shoulder for just long enough for them to feel the shame of their actions.

In the sheltered spinning and knitting workshops, the young girls of York were protected while learning a trade, and many went on to being placed as servants into creditable families, rather than falling into vice and infamy.

Resources

One of the best resources for finding out if your ancestor was a member of a club or association are the historical newspapers from their time and place. Often, meetings or gatherings would be reported on and it is quite common to find listings of attendees within the articles. Searching by surname and place is recommended since the articles often refer to the members by their title within the organization such as 'Brother Watson'.

For the most part, very early records of clubs and associations such as the Foresters, the Masons or the Oddfellows are not extant, either because records were never created, because they were not preserved or simply because membership in the earliest years was often secret.

Despite that, some late eighteenth and nineteenth century records for the Foresters Friendly society do exist and have been gathered and are available at the AOF Heritage Trust office in South Hampton who accept research enquiries. The Library and Museum of Freemasonry website also has a few links to online resources, one of which is the Lane's Masonic Records website that lists all the Masonic Lodges from

1717 to 1894. In addition, Ancestry hold records of the Grand Lodge of Freemasons of Ireland from 1733 to 1923. The Oddfellows have their own website and a pay-per-view online searchable archive, as well as a brief history of their inception. Links to all the resources mentioned can be found in the appendix.

With the sheer number of fraternities, clubs and associations that were in existence in the time of our ancestors, it is impossible to list resources for them all. The best way to find more information about the organization your ancestor belonged to is to do a web search for '<association> England history' or to enquire at the local county record office.

MARKETS AND FAIRS

As genealogists, we are accustomed to researching our ancestors' occupations and learning about their work but we often neglect to familiarize ourselves with what they might have done in their leisure hours. Just as today, our ancestors liked to have a good time and would have enjoyed local markets and fairs with their family, friends and neighbours.

The earliest markets and fairs were held either by Royal Grant, or simply by long custom. Although similar in nature, markets and fairs can be distinguished by how often they were held. Markets were regular trading events, often held weekly, while fairs were normally annual events held at the same time each year, often on a patron saint's day. Local fairs and markets would have been augmented with larger venues in nearby towns where farmers and cottage artisans could show and sell their wares, a necessity in England's early economy. Occasionally, Royal Charters would be granted for even bigger events and the result would be a very large fair with international merchants in attendance at the fair which might run for as long as four weeks.

By the late eighteenth century, several Acts of Parliament had been passed to make sure that fairs were, pardon the play on words, fair for all. Organizers were required to measure out the designated amount of open space for the use of the merchants attending the fair. They were allowed to charge a toll for all horses that were brought into the grounds but were required to record the details in a ledger for that purpose. Sales of livestock were to be accompanied by a bill of sale, detailing the arrangement. Weights and measures were dictated and the only acceptable measurement was the 'Winchester bushel' which contained eight gallons. Disputes were dealt with quickly, according to predetermined rules and fines for ignoring the rules were steep, the proceeds of which would be split between the informer and the poor of the parish.

The fairs in the days of our ancestors were held not only to serve the needs of the local area but the larger ones attracted merchants and traders from further away, and many merchants made a living by travelling from one fair to another, buying goods in one place and selling them in another. As well as serving as a place of trade for livestock, fairs also served as an opportunity for the servants in the area to find new employment for the following year, and often attracted travelling shows and peddlers of novelties for the amusement of the attendees.

By the mid-nineteenth century, the coming of the railways to many market towns had greatly eroded patronage of the fairs and at the same time, the auction market had lessened the need for the agricultural fairs by affording the farmers with a steady and frequent outlet for their produce.

Case Study – Northallerton Markets

Farmers in the eighteenth century depended on markets and fairs to sell their livestock and would have typically attended such an event close to their property. This case study looks at a farmer who lived in the Northallerton area in this period and the local fairs and markets at that time using land records, newspapers and the published account of fairs written by William Owen in 1788.

In 1787, when William Bulmer, yeoman, purchased Streetlam Castle Farm near Danby Wiske, Yorkshire from William Wrightson, it consisted of arable meadows and pastures and the following year, he made yet a further agreement for grazing rights on the Outhwaite Moor, making it clear he raised at least some livestock.

Most likely, when it came time to buy or sell his cattle and horses,

William Bulmer would have attended the fair held in nearby Northallerton, just over six miles from his land.

The fairs in Northallerton were normally held on Candlemas Day, St George's, St Bartholomew's and St Mathew's Day and the day before the fair day was designated as the show-day. The tradition of a fair in Northallerton dated back to the year 1200 when King John granted a charter to Philip de Poicteu, the Bishop of Durham. In the early years, the fair might last as long as a month but by the mid-nineteenth century, it had been shortened to about a week with most of the horses having been bought even before the fair commenced.

Farmers would bring their horned cattle, their horses and sheep to the fairs to sell or trade. Northallerton was also the site for horse racing and horses that won at the races there commanded high prices for stud or for sale. The fairs, held near the church, often drew traders from as far away as Northumbria and Scotland and local merchants would bring their products to sell, including such fripperies as pins, silken laces, knives, combs, scissors, and thimbles for the ladies.

In addition to the four annual fairs, there was a market held every other Wednesday for the sale of live cattle. On the second Wednesday in October, a market was held for the sale of cheese and the regular market day was held each Wednesday for corn and similar provisions.

Further afield were the fairs held in York, a distance of just over thirty-five miles from William Bulmer's home Streetlam. They were held the Thursday before Palm Sunday, on Whitsun Monday, 10 July, 12 August, 22 November and every other Thursday throughout the year. There was a half-year fair that was primarily for horses and the summer fair was held during race-week, when more visitors would attend. The winter fair was held on a Monday in mid-December and would last the first whole week before Christmas.

Similarly, a fair was held in Leeds: on 10 July for horses and hardware, on October 8 and every Monday fortnight for cattle and 8 November for horned cattle, horses and hardware, but that was fifty miles away, a distance which would have taken almost a full day of travel by horse and carriage.

The coming of the railway in the nineteenth century all but put an end to the great livestock fairs in Yorkshire. By then, William Bulmer's Streetlam farm had passed to his son Thomas after his death in 1825.

Resources

For the earliest history of markets and fairs in England, there is an online database, The Gazetteer of Markets and Fairs in England and Wales to 1516, hosted by the University of London. For later fairs, the 1788 volume by William Owen entitled the *New Book of Fairs* is available in digitized format on the Internet Archive.

Details of fairs and markets are to be found in newspaper articles from your ancestors' time and place. Expect to find listings of the types and number of animals that were offered for sale or bought and the prices they commanded.

Follow in your ancestors' footsteps. Some fairs, such as The Goose Fair of Nottinghamshire, have been running more or less every year dating back to medieval times. The Goose Fair boasts over 700 years of history with most historians agreeing the fair probably began just after 1284 although it was cancelled in 1646 during the bubonic plague and again briefly during the First and Second World Wars. Although now famous for its carnival rides, it was once known for trade opportunities, especially in cheese. The fair was once held in Market Square in the centre of Nottingham, but was moved to the Forest Recreation Ground early in the twentieth century. Why not make plans to attend?

EDUCATION, LANGUAGE AND LITERACY

By 1700, only 40 per cent of men and 25 per cent of women were able to sign their own name at the time of their marriage, although this in itself was not necessarily a sign of literacy. Towards the middle of the eighteenth century, however, many factors came into play that resulted in an improvement of the reading and writing abilities of our ancestors. In 1710, the Statute of Anne, also known as the Copyright Act, was passed by Parliament. Prior to the passage of this Act, the Stationers' Company, one of the livery companies of London, held a monopoly over the publishing industry in England, but the act of 1710 broke the stranglehold of the London publishers. It introduced a copyright term of fourteen years for authors, rather than publishers, and paved the way for the establishment of publishing companies throughout England. The printed word became more readily available outside the capital and less expensive. As a result, an increasing number of our ancestors could afford books.

At the same time, in the late eighteenth century, the Sunday School movement began to catch hold in England. Working children, freed

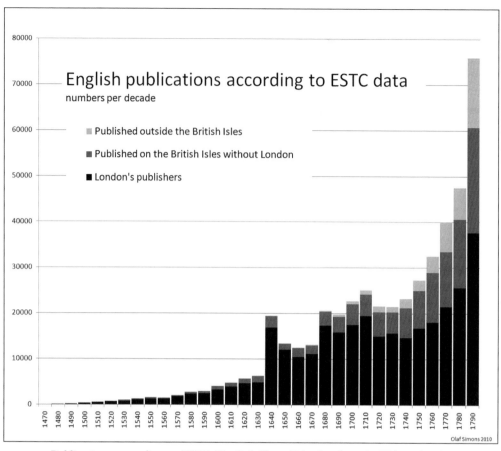

Publications according to ESTC (English Short Title Catalogue). (Wikimedia CC 3.0)

from their labours at the factories on Sundays, would attend private or church schools on Sundays to learn how to read and write. Robert Raikes, the editor of the *Gloucester Journal*, is credited as a pioneer in the movement, although he did not himself start a school, but he published accounts of the schools established in his community. Inspired by Raikes, William Fox formed the Sunday School Society in 1785, garnering the support of leading philanthropists of the time and the group met regularly at the Paul's Head Tavern in London. By 1788, the society had established and assisted 333 schools throughout England helping to educate more than 21,000 students, and supplied the schools with spelling books, testaments and bibles. By 1831, Sunday schools in Britain were teaching 1,250,000 children weekly and the idea of public education was gaining ground.

It was not until 1870, however, that education became mandatory in England and Wales. With the passage of the Elementary Education Act on 17 February 1870, school boards were formed to provide schools for children between the ages of 5 and 13. By 1880, attendance was mandatory up to the age of 10, but it was not until the Education Act of 1891 that state schools became essentially free, with Parliament financing the elementary schools in England and Wales by way of a grant for each attending student. In 1893, the leaving age rose to 13.

In 1902, the Conservative Education Act resulted in sweeping changes to the education landscape in England and Wales. Local education authorities were established, replacing the School Boards that had administered the public schools up until that time, and brought funding to the 14,000 church schools.

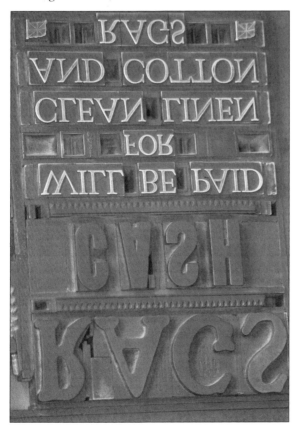

The printing press revolutionized the written word.

As genealogists and social history researchers, we need to remember our earlier ancestors who were employed as farmers, blacksmiths, masons and in other traditional occupations had no great need to know how to read or write and even if they had been taught to do so early in life, their abilities diminished over time with lack of use. It wasn't until the nineteenth century that the printed word truly became a part of everyday life.

Case Study – Burslem School Attendance Officer

Although school attendance to age 10 became compulsory in 1880, the School Boards and attendance officers frequently had to battle just to keep the children in school. This case study looks at the Burslem School Board reports from 1880 using articles in the Staffordshire newspaper and follows the career of one of the attendance officers using basic genealogical records.

Although there were 6,396 pupils on the books of the Burslem School Board, the average attendance in 1880 was only 4,582 or 71 per cent. This was, however, a marked improvement from when the school board had initially launched six years earlier. In the first year, the board had 3,317 students registered but an average attendance of only 1,967 or 59 per cent. The improved attendance over the past six years was due in some part to parents giving education a greater importance but much of the credit for the better attendance was owed to the two attendance officers employed by the Burslem Board.

Attendance officer Frederick Davenport, himself the father of three school-age children, had inquired after 582 absences or irregular attendees and his partner, Mr Bailey, the second attendance officer, had inquired after 482 absences during the same period. Close to half of the missing children were said to have been sick, although whether they were or not might have been open to question. Nearly 256 students, or 20 per cent, were absent due to their parent's negligence, and this often resulted in a summons to court and a 5-shilling fine. About 10 per cent of the students were needed at home and another 10 per cent were sent home because they had not paid the fees. Only 38 students or 3 per cent were playing truant. The rest

---

had left the district, had gone to work or had been kept home due to bad weather.

Monitoring attendance at the school was of particularly importance since the schools were awarded grant money based on the number of students who attended at a rate of 15s 9d per head which accounted for about 43 per cent of the cost of their education. The rest was met by the school rates of 8s 7d per child with the remaining being charged in fees of approximately 11s per student each term. Those parents who simply couldn't afford the fees had the option of applying to the Board of Guardians for assistance.

Frederick Davenport retires, Staffordshire Advertiser, *Saturday 2 August 1919.*

Frederick Davenport, the attendance officer for Burslem in 1880, had himself gone to work in a factory at the age of 8, working as a glass cutter for sixteen years before being appointed as the school attendance officer in 1873. He continued in that capacity until 1885 when he was appointed as the Relieving Officer for Burslem, working tirelessly on behalf of the poor of Burslem for another thirty-four years. He regretfully retired from that position in August 1919 and died on 4 October 1925.

Frederick Davenport's four sons, John, Thomas, William and James, were no doubt inspired by their father's example, and attended school until the leaving age. Thomas became a Minister with the Methodist Free Church and James became the Deputy & Assistant Registrar of births, marriages and deaths. William ran his own business as carting contractor and John became a coal merchant.

Resources

Many of the traditional genealogy records such as marriage records and probate records bear your ancestors' signatures. Look for the original record or a high-quality copy. Just because your ancestor made their mark instead of signing their name, it does not necessarily mean they could not write. They may have made their mark on the marriage record rather than signing their name so as not to embarrass their partner who could not sign or may have simply followed the instructions given them by the minister.

Some school registers and log books have survived and are most likely to be found in local archives. Selected National School records between 1870 and 1914 have been digitized and are available to search on Findmypast and the admissions and discharge registers for London schools from 1840 to 1911 are on Ancestry. Even if your ancestor is not included, browsing the images can give a fascinating glimpse into the schools of the past.

Another great resource for educational records is the School Records website. This site has information about where to find school records including registers and admission books online. The website also has links to several local school record indexing projects by various family history organizations.

Finally, as with most social history research, don't neglect historical newspapers when researching your ancestors' education. It is common to find notices of school awards, graduating classes or achievements in the local newspaper. For those of us with ancestors who were not especially fond of school, there are also notices of truants and of parents who were brought up on charges for failing to send their children to school.

RELIGION AND CHURCH

From 1534 when Henry VIII broke with Rome, both religion and politics went through a tumultuous time, with Catholicism and Protestantism gaining and losing favour even as the monarchy battled with Parliament for control of the country. Three years after Henry's break with Rome, a law was passed requiring that baptisms, marriages and burials taking place in the Church of England must be recorded in the parish registers. Religion and the church began to mark the passage of our ancestors' lives.

Although the Church of England was the established church, some of our ancestors were Nonconformists. Early Dissenters were the Presbyterians, Baptists, Independents, Catholics, Quakers and the

Huguenots and later, the Methodists. From 1754, with the passage of Hardwicke's Act, all marriages had to take place in the Church of England to be legal, regardless of the bride and groom's religion, with the exception of Quakers and Jews. It wasn't until the Marriage Act of 1836 that Nonconformist ministers, including Roman Catholic priests, were allowed to register marriages and civil marriages became legal.

Most burials also took place in Church of England burial grounds until public cemeteries were established beginning in the early nineteenth century. The new burial places were driven not only by public health concerns about the overcrowded church burial grounds but by a growing number of people in dissenting religions who preferred not to be buried on lands belonging to the Church of England.

In 1851, when the religious census was taken, it revealed that less than 30 per cent of the population attended Church of England services while almost as many regularly attended other Christian churches. It was estimated there were over 34,000 places of worship in England and Wales on 30 March 1851 and with morning, afternoon and evening services available, there was theoretically seating for more than 20 million people to attend. In reality, however, because of the uneven distribution of the churches across England, the densely-populated towns had a scarcity of seats for the large volume of worshipers, even though the number of churches had almost doubled since the beginning of the nineteenth century.

One of the factors contributing to the shortage of seats for worshipers in the Church of England was the common practice of pew rental fees for parishioners as a means of raising money. This practice became controversial in the mid-nineteenth century and a growing movement for 'free and open churches' resulted in the abolishment of pew rents through the remainder of the century.

Regardless of what faith your ancestor belonged to, or whether they were part of a small rural parish or a large urban one, it is likely that the church was a foundation in their lives.

Case Study – St Philips Church, Sheffield

In 1818, Parliament passed the first Church Building Act, establishing a grant of £1 million pounds to be used to build new churches to accommodate the masses of people who flocked to the cities in the industrial revolution. St. Philips Church in Sheffield was one of the churches built from the fund. This case study is about the act, the church and its history and uses newspaper articles and the 1851 Ecclesiastical Census as resources.

By the beginning of the nineteenth century, Sheffield, with its population of over 60,000 people, had a serious problem. There were only three Church of England churches in the town St Peter's, now the Cathedral, was ancient, the building dating back to 1280. In the eighteenth century, two more churches were erected. St Paul's was built by subscription in 1721 and St James was built by pew proprietary in 1789. In addition, there were three ancient chapels at Attercliffe, Ecclesall and the Shrewsbury Hospital. But in all, there were only pews for 6,280 people, quite a serious deficiency in the growing city.

Sheffield was not the only city suddenly bursting with an incoming population. All over England, the Industrial Revolution had sparked a mass migration of people from rural communities to the cities, as they searched for employment in the manufactories that sprung up seemingly overnight. Like Sheffield, Stockport, Manchester and other northern cities had outgrown their ancient churches and were also in desperate need. In recognition, Parliament voted in 1818 to establish a grant of £1 million to build new churches and established the Church Building Commission to manage the fund. The programme was extended with a further grant of £500,000 in 1824

By 1820, the population of Sheffield stood at almost 85,000 people and the city was still growing rapidly. It would increase fivefold by the end of the century. On 28 March 1820 in the vestry of Sheffield Parish Church a meeting was held, chaired by the Reverend Thomas Sutton, and it was decided that three churches should be built under the Act (although ultimately four were built). These were Attercliffe, St George's, St Mary's and St Philip's.

The foundation stone for St Philips was laid on 26 September 1822 shortly after noon on the property donated by Philip Gell, Esq. of Hopton, Derbyshire. The building site of one acre and two roods was at the foot of Shalesmoor, between Infirmary Road and Penistone Road near the Infirmary. The architect, Mr Taylor of Leeds, designed a gothic style building that was 95 feet long and 78 feet wide at a cost of £11,960, funded out of the Parliamentary grant provided by the Church Building Commission. When completed, St. Philips added an additional 2,000 pews for public worship in Sheffield although subsequent renovations in later years to add choir stalls and a vestry would reduce that to 1850 pews.

By Sunday, 30 March 1851, when the Ecclesiastical Census was taken, the total population of Sheffield had swelled to over 135,000 people and although a third of these were now Methodists or Wesleyans, some 44 per cent of the population still attended the Church of England. At St Philips, 650 parishioners came to the morning services to hear Rev John Livesey preach, 160 scholars attended the Sunday School and a further 600 parishioners attended the evening service. Despite the fact that when Rev Livesey filled out the census return that day, he commented 'This fine church has been greatly and permanently injured by inattention to the principals of acoustics in its construction', over 75 per cent of the available pews had been filled.

The church remained as the spiritual centre of the neighbourhood until it was damaged during the Second World War and was finally torn down in the 1950s.

Resources

The laws of church and state in England are interwoven, especially where marriage is concerned. A summary of the significant changes to the marriage laws over time can be found on the Parliament website by searching 'law of marriage' from the home page. The laws about burials can be found at the Legislation website by searching 'burial act' from the home page. There have been many scholarly articles and books written on the history of religious groups, parishes and churches in England. Search for these online using your favourite search engine.

The religious census of 1851 for England, Wales and Scotland was a controversial survey taken only once, on the night of 30 March 1851, and never repeated. Its stated purpose was to evaluate whether or not the number of seats or pews in the churches had kept up with the increased population. Reporting was not mandatory, although 34,467 forms were filled in by ministers across the country in some form of completeness and these individual returns can be downloaded from the National Archives. A comprehensive report, *Census of Great Britain, 1851: Religious Worship in England and Wales* was prepared to summarize the results of the unique census and was released in 1854. The book can be viewed on the Internet Archive.

Parish registers and bishops' transcripts are records that we as genealogists use frequently to find the names, dates and places that relate to our ancestors but these documents can also provide an insight into the history of the church and the parish. When searching microfilmed copies of the register, be sure to take a look at the pages at the beginning and end of the book, since these sometimes contain notes made by the parish priest about various aspects of the church. I have found parish histories, pew assignments, budgets for renovations and other ad hoc entries on such pages. In addition to the records of baptism, marriages and burials, the parish chest records, if they survive, can offer a wealth of information about the parish and its history.

As always, search historical newspapers for the church your ancestor attended. You can expect to find notices and descriptions of church and social events as well as details of fundraising for the poor. The building and opening of churches built in the nineteenth century are often detailed as are changes in clergy and news events involving the church.

PERSECUTION

Persecution is defined as 'hostility and ill-treatment, especially because of race or political or religious beliefs' and no doubt, many of our ancestors either suffered persecution or witnessed it in their daily lives in one degree or another.

Jewish people, who appear to have arrived in England around the time of the Norman Conquest in 1066 were initially welcomed and were considered direct subjects of the King in the feudal system of the time. They were allowed to move about the country at will and often became moneylenders since the established church forbade the lending of money for profit, a restriction that did not apply to Jews. When some of the Jewish moneylenders became quite wealthy, the King, as was his right, heavily taxed them and during the thirteenth century alone, forty-nine separate levies were imposed upon them, putting vast sums of money into the pockets of the Crown. After Edward I returned from the Crusades in 1274, he passed the Statute of the Jewry, making money-lending for interest illegal and ordered that all Jewish people over the age of 12 had to wear a yellow badge on their clothing. Although allowed to make a living as merchants, farmers and craftsmen, many of the Jews continued to lend money secretly and finally, in 1290, Edward expelled the Jewish community and they were not allowed to return until the late seventeenth century.

Beginning in the sixteenth and seventeenth centuries, after King Henry broke from Rome, the Catholic community was also increasingly persecuted for their religious beliefs. They were excluded from society, were denied the privilege of holding any sort of office and were heavily taxed. In some cases, their land was even seized, all sanctioned by the Crown. Being a priest or celebrating mass was a crime punishable by death.

The Puritans, a group of reformed Protestants who supported the anti-Catholic movement, sought to remove all 'popish' customs from the Church of England, claiming the Reformation had not gone far enough. When Charles I became King in 1625, the conflict surrounding the reformation of the Church intensified and in 1630, an assembly of dissenting Puritans left England for Massachusetts Bay in the new world and this migration continued over the course of the next decade. Those who stayed behind in England, however, became a force to reckon with after the first English Civil War that took place between 1642 and 1646. Following the restoration of the monarchy in 1660 and the passage of the Act of Uniformity in 1662, the Puritans fell from power and many became Nonconformists, breaking with the established church.

Even today, all around the globe, to be different often means being ostracized from society, or even actively persecuted. It was no different in our ancestors' time. Those of different religions, races and beliefs were at the very least regarded with suspicion and held at arm's length, and often denied the rights and privileges of the majority.

Case Study – The Gordon Riots

In 1780, riots and looting broke out in London in protest against the Papists Act of 1778. This case study is about the Gordon Riots, as they came to be called, and looks at public sentiment at the time. It uses newspaper articles and other general resources.

From the sixteenth century when Henry VIII broke with Rome, Catholics had been discriminated against, even persecuted in England. They were prohibited from voting, from holding a seat in Parliament and from attending the universities. From 1571, it was a treasonable offence to support the Pope or engage in any form of Catholic worship, the penalty for which was execution by being hanged, drawn and quartered. Between 1580 and about 1680 many priests who were caught saying mass or engaging in other 'popish' activities were executed and the Catholic community survived only in secret congregations throughout England.

At the outbreak of the American War of Independence in 1775, the British Army consisted of only about 45,000 men who were spread across the globe throughout the colonies. By 1778, England's armed forces were stretched thin, fighting not only in the newly-formed United States of America but also in France and Spain. To augment their forces, England engaged German mercenaries, but this was insufficient to the growing demand.

In 1778, Parliament passed the Papists Act which excused Catholics from taking a religious oath when joining the British Army, thus paving the way to increase the numbers of Catholics in the military. In addition, the Act allowed Catholics to own property and inherit land and the section of law that had allowed the executions of priests in the sixteenth and seventeenth century was repealed. Catholic schools were no longer outlawed and books related to the Catholic faith were no longer forbidden.

With the passage of the Papists Act, anti-Catholic sentiment was ignited amongst the public and open letters to Parliament appeared in the newspapers to repeal the new law. In January 1780, the *Caledonian Mercury* printed one such petition: 'That Popish Bishops, Priests, Jesuits and Schoolmasters now openly exercise their functions, whereby the people, especially the rising generation, are in danger of being led into superstition, idolatry and rebellion.'

By summer, when Parliament refused to repeal the act, the people of London took to the street. On Friday, 2 June, a large crowd estimated at 50,000 people assembled in St George's Fields. Led by Lord George Gordon, the President of the Protestant Association of London, the crowd marched on the House of Parliament carrying banners calling for 'No Popery'. Gordon entered the House and presented their petition for repeal of the 1778 Act, but it was quickly dismissed with a decisive vote. Outside, the crowd began to riot, but were eventually dispersed by a detachment of soldiers and authorities believed that order had been restored.

But the protest was not over. That night, crowds attacked chapels throughout the city and vandalized the homes of known Catholics. A reward of £500 was offered by King George for information leading to the arrest of any of the rioters, with a promise of immunity from prosecution. The following night, in the slums of Moorfields, a crowd gathered once more. Newgate Prison was attacked and destroyed as was 'The Clink', and many prisoners were set free. Catholic homes, chapels and several embassies were damaged or destroyed. Over 300 people died during the rioting, most shot by the army who was finally called in to restore order on 7 June, and property damage was extensive. About 450 rioters were arrested, with twenty to thirty eventually being tried and executed for their part in the riot.

Lord George Gordon himself was arrested on 9 June 1780 and charged with high treason. He was committed to the Tower of London to await trial. During the trial which began in early January 1781, the prosecutors failed to prove Gordon had any treasonable intent, and he was acquitted.

Resources

For those with ancestors who were part of one of the minority groups throughout England's history, there are often specialty historical or genealogical societies who focus on those particular areas of social history. The Huguenot Society offers members journals and specialty publications, all relating to the history of the Huguenot families. Likewise, the Catholic Family History Society offers publications related to Catholic history and transcriptions of early Catholic records to their members.

For those with Jewish ancestry, especially between the eighteenth and twentieth centuries, the National Archives has a research guide listing the diverse set of records in their collection. For the most extensive and comprehensive collection of documents on the early London Jewish community, visit the London Metropolitan Archives. The Charles Booth Online Archive has digitized versions of four of Booth's notebooks relating to the Jewish community in London in the 1880s and 1890s.

Since the religious debates from the sixteenth century onwards are closely interwoven with the political upheavals during the period, much context for religious and ethnic persecution can be found in historical accounts of related events such as the Reformation, the Jacobite Rebellion and the Civil War.

As always, search the many digitized books on Google Books and the Internet Archive for accounts of the various minority groups throughout England's history and read the historical newspapers to gauge both public opinion and political controversies that surrounded these groups.

CRIME AND PUNISHMENT

As we move further back in time, criminals were paradoxically at once both more and less harshly dealt with than in the present, in accordance with the social mores of the time. The attitudes and tolerances of society change with the passage of years and the trial books of the Old Bailey court reflect these fluctuations in public judgements.

On the one hand, some crimes considered as particularly heinous in our time were viewed differently in the past. In 1715, when William Cash found himself in court accused of raping a 12-year-old servant girl when his wife was away, he defended himself by saying that although he had thrown the young girl on the bed and tried to have his way with her, he was unsuccessful in completing the act. When his story was confirmed by two medical men, he was acquitted of the charge and set free.

And yet, on the other hand, young children were often arrested and convicted, forced to serve time in the crowded prisons amongst the adults, transported or branded for crimes as trivial and perhaps as understandable as stealing a crust of bread to eat. In 1690, young

William Carter, a 10-year-old boy, was brought to the Old Bailey for stealing two gold rings and a few gold coins. When the charges were fully proved, he was found guilty of grand larceny and was branded on the hand. Similarly, in 1784, when 12-year-old Joseph Magginnis was found guilty of stealing a single linen handkerchief valued at four pence, he was whipped by the hangman for his transgression. That the whipping was carried out privately was perhaps the only concession to his tender age.

Looking back to the eighteenth century, many crimes were considered capital offences, punishable by death. Some of these, as could be expected, were murder, treason and highway robbery but others seem more like misdemeanours such as cutting down a tree, robbing a rabbit warren and damaging London Bridge. From 1735 to 1799, over 6,000 people were executed for their crimes, most of them men, but some women also faced the ultimate penalty. In the nineteenth century, the number of capital offences was reduced, and the number of those executed fell to less than 4,000. Hanging was by far the most common execution method but throughout history, some were drawn and quartered, burned alive or even hanged in chains until dead. As an alternative to death, many of the convicted were transported, first to America and later to Australia, either for a set period, or sometimes for life.

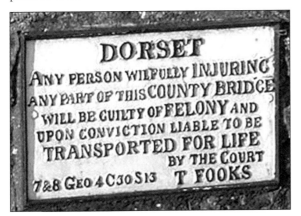

A notice on Sturminster Newton bridge. Taken by Steinsky, July 2004.

Until 1868, when they were moved indoors, executions were public events, and the majority of the hangings in England were carried out at the village of Tyburn, just outside of London. The eight 'hanging days'

173

of the year in Tyburn were popular with the public and always drew a large, boisterous crowd of spectators, often 30,000 strong.

Did any of your ancestors run afoul of the law? What was their crime and how were they punished? Even if your ancestors were all law-abiding citizens, it is likely their lives were somehow affected by crime and punishment in their time.

Case Study – Pleading their Bellies

Women who were convicted of capital crimes such as coining and were sentenced to hang could 'plead their bellies' and avoid the hangman's noose for a time, and sometimes permanently. The study uses the records from the Old Bailey website and other general resources to look at the case of Mary Nash.

Mary Nash was indicted for theft on 21 February 1733 at the Old Bailey. It was claimed she had stolen a brass box and three shillings from Jane, the wife of Thomas Ordway the previous day, but when Mrs Ordway failed to appear in court, she was acquitted. Seven years later, almost to the day, she was back in court, indicted on 27 February 1740 for assaulting George Stacey at the house of William Needham, and for stealing his Portuguese Moidore gold coin worth about thirty-six shillings, as well as thirty guineas.

Mary Nash, along with Elizabeth Whitney, alias Dribray, had met the victim in the street about 8 o'clock in the evening and asked him to buy them a drink. They proceeded to Needham's house, the Rose, and had three quarterns of gin but after the drinks were finished, they asked Stacey for money. He gave them two sixpence and paid for the drinks but when he rose to leave, they held him by his arms and forced him down, gagging him, and assaulting him.

Stacey testified that Nash and Whitney took at least thirty guineas from him and his Moidore gold coin and fled, leaving him bleeding on the floor. When he raised the alarm, help came and his rescuers found the two women. Mary Nash, when apprehended, had twenty-five guineas in her bosom and another in her hair. There was no sign of the Moidore coin.

Sarah Scot, who found the victim, collaborated his testimony, saying she arrived as Nash and Whitney were picking his pockets.

She turned and ran to Mr Bird, the fishmonger, shouting to him that a man was being killed at the Rose and he told her to fetch the constable. She hurried back to the Rose and met the two women leaving and tried to stop them. A scuffle ensued and Stacey came to help Scot and eventually the accused were in their custody.

Elizabeth Whitney claimed she had not stolen any money, but that it had been Mary Nash who had taken the coin from George Stacey's pocket. For her part, Mary Nash said Stacey had offered them money if they would have a drink with him.

Several witnesses came forward to testify to the character of Mary Nash saying she was a gloveress, whose husband had sold pictures but had left her and gone to sea, saying that she was of good character. Elizabeth Whitney's father testified he had not had much to do with his daughter in many years but she worked in dressmaking making Mantua robes, and he knew little about her life but that she was just and honest.

Both Mary Nash and Elizabeth Whitney were found guilty of their crimes and were sentenced to death and committed to Newgate to await their punishment. Elizabeth Whitney was scheduled to be hanged at Tyburn on Wednesday, 7 May 1740, but at the last moment, her sentence was commuted to transportation for life by the King and she was transported to Virginia in May 1740 aboard the *Essex*.

Mary Nash 'pled the belly' and when examined by a jury of matrons, it was found she was indeed quick with child. She was held over to the next sessions, pending the birth of her baby. On 21 March 1741, having given birth, the case of Mary Nash was one of those brought to the King at the Council at St James's and he graciously pardoned her from execution as well, commuting her sentence to transportation for life.

Mary Nash was transported to Maryland aboard either the *Speedwell* or the *Mediterranean* which sailed from England in April 1741. The fate of her child is unknown.

Resources

There are many excellent resources available to the social historian interested in crime and punishment. The proceedings of the Old Bailey, London's central criminal court, are available online in a searchable

Being put in the pillory was a very public punishment. (Public domain)

database with accounts of trials between 1674 and 1913, an excellent resource and detailed social history accounts that draws almost 200,000 visits each year.

Ancestry has a criminal records database covering the period from 1791 to 1892, created from Home Office records from the National Archives. They also have several related databases containing information about convicts transported to Australia, New South Wales. Likewise, Findmypast also has a collection of criminal records including Prison Ship Registers, Metropolitan Police habitual criminal registers and others.

To find further information about those who were sentenced to transportation to Australia, there are several excellent resources. The Convict Records website has a searchable database for those transported between 1787 and 1867, and other, similar resources can be found by doing an online search for 'Australian convict databases'.

The York Family History Society hosts a searchable database of prisoners who were brought to trial at the York Assizes between 1785 and 1851 and the Crime and Punishment database at The National

Library of Wales website holds details of crimes tried at the Court of Great Sessions in Wales between 1730 and 1830.

Some crimes were so sensational that books were written about them. Search the various book collections for accounts such as *The Life and Adventures of Jack Sheppard*, an account of the crimes and prison escapes of an infamous robber and thief of the eighteenth century. Search historical newspapers for accounts of crimes and detailed court proceedings including witness statements and for coroner's inquests. Like in our time, crime is news, but unlike our time, there was little expectation of privacy and newspapers provided incredible details of crimes and trials ranging from the pettiest to the most sensational trials.

WAR, REVOLUTION AND UNREST

Wars, revolutions and unrest mark the pages of Britain's history from the earliest days to the present. Even during the period between 1815 and 1914, referred to as the 'Pax Britannica' and regarded as a period of relative peace in Europe and the world, there were many conflicts including the Crimean War that raged between 1854 and 1856, the Indian Mutiny of 1857 to 1859, and the Boer Wars of 1880 to 1881 and 1899 to 1902.

Historians have long studied the countless wars, revolutions and armed conflicts throughout history and detailed accounts of wars, battles and campaigns overflow the shelves of libraries. But as social historians, we are not focused on war itself as we are in the stories of the men, women and children touched by the ravages of war.

The military historians will note that in the Peninsular War, part of the Napoleonic Wars that lasted from 1807 to 1814, the British army lost 9,000 men in action and almost 25,000 more men from disease, and more than 30,000 men were wounded during the conflict. But we, as social historians, see each of those 64,000 men as husbands, fathers, sons or brothers, each with their own story to tell. We see the effects of the casualties on the wives, mothers, children and siblings who stayed at home. We see the impacts of the war on the social history of the time in the food shortages, in the children who didn't have enough to eat and in the wives who became dependant on the parish or who entered the workhouse just to survive. We imagine the heart-rending letters written home from the front and we see the family, friends and neighbours who came back broken, maimed or ill or who never came home at all.

Most of us will have at least one ancestor who went off to war, perhaps experiencing events that no one should have to experience and all of us will have ancestors who were affected by war, revolution or unrest in some form or another. Woven in between the campaigns, battles and offensives of the wars that touched our ancestors' lives are the human stories of real people. While the dates and places recorded in the history books form the framework of the narrative, the true story is that of the individual soldiers and their families and friends as they struggle to cope with a world that suddenly seems to have spun off its axis. What were your ancestors' stories?

Case Study – Wounded at Braklaagte

The Second Boer War in South Africa began on 11 October 1899 and ended on 31 May 1902 with the signing of the Treaty of Vereeniging. In June 1901, midway through the war, Arthur Roland George Wilberforce, the son of the Bishop of Chichester, was severely wounded in battle at Braklaagte. The study uses newspaper accounts and other general resources to look at the human side of the war.

Arthur Roland George Wilberforce was the oldest son of Ernest Roland Wilberforce, the Bishop of Chichester and the former Bishop of Newcastle. During his childhood, Arthur had lived with his family at the Bishop of Newcastle's residence at Benwell Towers to the west of Newcastle upon Tyne, where the household staff included a governess, a laundress and laundrymaid, two housemaids, a kitchen maid, a nursemaid and a footman. When he was nineteen, his father was appointed Bishop of Chichester and the family moved to The Palace in Chichester, another stately home that dated back to the twelfth century.

When 23-year-old Arthur volunteered for Paget's Horse of the Imperial Yeomanry in Liverpool on 30 January 1901, the Boer War in South Africa had been raging for over a year. The men who had enlisted in the first contingent of the Imperial Yeomanry had either been killed, invalided out or had reached the end of their twelve-month service and were returning home. The intense recruiting efforts for the second contingent had raised over 16,000 men and by early February they were shipped off to South Africa, poorly trained but urgently needed.

Less than six months after Arthur enlisted, the Paget Horse, along with the 7th Dragoon Guards, were engaged in a rearguard action with the Boers at Braklaagte on 4 June. The battle was intense and Arthur's commanding officer, Lieutenant Charles W. Hulse was killed, along with Captain W.M. Lonfield of the 41st Company and many were wounded, Arthur among them.

It wasn't until late June that the Bishop of Chichester received word that his son, Trooper A.R.G. Wilberforce had been dangerously wounded during the battle at Braklaagte. After several anxious days, the family received notice Arthur was making favourable progress. When Arthur had recovered enough to put pen to paper, he wrote a letter to his father describing the battle.

'An officer dashed in with the order, "Retire at all costs, and leave the wounded," and we were left lying where we were,' he wrote. As the British troops withdrew, the Boers rushed in, stripping the wounded of their possessions, one even trying to pull the ring from the finger of Arthur's injured arm. After pillaging all they could from the battlefield, the Boers set the veldt on fire to cover their retreat, Arthur explained, and the flames 'approached us with a roar'. The flames were within 40 feet, he said, when the British troops were finally able to rush through the fire to rescue the wounded and carry them to safety.

It was not until August that Arthur had recovered sufficiently to be shipped safely home and he arrived back at the Bishop's Palace on the evening of 18 August, welcomed by his mother, brothers and sisters at the railway station.

Resources

There is a plethora of books and online resources dedicated to the study of military history that trace the movements of troops across the battlefields and detail the engagements of the various armies, navies and later the air forces. These can be found in any library or through a simple web search. Use these to outline your ancestor's story.

Fill in some of the personal details using the military records available both on free websites and on the paid subscription websites such as Ancestry and Findmypast. Free websites include the Anglo-Boer War website and Families in British India Society or FIBIS but many others can be found across the internet.

Finally, colour in your military ancestor's portrait by learning more about what their experience was like by reading contemporary letters, diaries, and other personal accounts. If your ancestor did not leave any personal papers, read those of others with similar stories on websites such as the First World War website. Find more diaries and letters by using a search term such as '<Your War> diaries and letters' to search the internet or the websites hosting out of print digitized books.

Historical newspapers will give a day-by-day account of the war, although news from the front was sometimes delayed by the technology of the time, but take the time to search for more personal stories. Who were the men that were killed? Did your ancestor lose any close friends or neighbours?

CONCLUSION

As genealogists, we seek to trace our familial lines back through the centuries by applying the principles of the Genealogical Proof Standard. We perform a reasonably exhaustive search for evidence, cite our sources, analyse and correlate the information we find while always resolving conflicts within the evidence and finally we present our conclusions in the form of pedigree charts and family group sheets. The results of our labours are the names, dates and places of our ancestors in chronological progression back through time.

But as social historians, we seek not only the names, dates and places, but the stories of our ancestors. By setting our ancestors against the backdrop of social history, we personify them, revealing their lives through the rich tapestry of details of their time and place. We see them as real people, long-lost relatives who lived and died long before we had a chance to know them, and yet, through the magic of research, we can introduce them to our families and preserve their memory for our descendants.

Which of your ancestors are you going to socialize with first?

BIBLIOGRAPHY OF RESOURCES

Resources located behind a paywall are designated with the symbol '£'. These paid resources are often available free of charge at libraries, archives and family history centres.

CHAPTER 1: INTRODUCTION

Thomas, Hugh. *A History of the World*. (New York: Harper & Row, 1979). Print.

Kurlansky, Mark. *Salt: A World History*. (Toronto: Vintage Canada, 2002). Print.

Digitized Books and Journals

Google Books: books.google.co.uk
Internet Archive: archive.org
Europeana: europeana.eu
Hathi Trust Digital Library: hathitrust.org
Project Gutenberg: gutenberg.org
Open Library: openlibrary.org
Family Search Books: books.familysearch.org
British Library Links to eBooks:
     www.bl.uk/reshelp/findhelprestype/webres/rarefacsimile/
Wellcome Library: wellcomelibrary.org
Archive CD Books Britain: archivecdbooks.ie
jStor: jstor.org
Internet Library of Early Journals: bodley.ox.ac.uk/ilej
British History Online: british-history.ac.uk

Print Books

World Cat: worldcat.org
eBay: ebay.co.uk

Images, Audio and Video
Internet Archive: archive.org
Europeana: europeana.eu
British Library Sounds: sounds.bl.uk
Wikimedia Commons: commons.wikimedia.org
YouTube: youtube.com
UK Copyright Service: copyrightservice.co.uk

Maps and Gazetteers
Old Maps: old-maps.co.uk
Old Maps Online: oldmapsonline.org
Vision of Britain Maps: visionofbritain.org.uk/maps
British Library Fire Insurance Maps: bl.uk/onlinegallery/onlineex/
    firemaps/fireinsurancemaps.html
Genuki Gazetteer: genuki.org.uk/big/Gazetteer/

Research Papers, Reports and Statistics
Vision of Britain Statistics: visionofbritain.org.uk/unit/10001043
Welton, Thomas Abercrombie. *Statistical Papers Base on the Census of
    England and Wales, 1851: And Relating to the Occupations of the People
    and the Increase of Population, 1841-51*. Google Books. (London:
    Printed for the Author by Savill and Edwards, 1860).
Google Scholar: scholar.google.co.uk
One-Place Studies: one-place-studies.org

Letters and Diaries
Dr Lucas Diaries: thedrlucasediaries.wordpress.com
Thompson, M. *Sailor's Letters Written to his Select Friends in England
    During His Voyages and Travels in Europe, Asia, Africa and America
    from the Year 1754 to 1759*. Google Books. (London: Printed for T.
    Becket and P.A. Dehondt in the Strand; W. Flexney, in Halbourn;
    and C. Moran, in Covent-Garden, 1767). bit.ly/SailorsLetters

Newspapers
£ British Newspaper Archive: britishnewspaperarchive.co.uk
£ Findmypast: findmypast.co.uk
The Gazette: thegazette.co.uk
National Library of Australia Trove: trove.nla.gov.au
Chronicling America: chroniclingamerica.loc.gov

Websites
Cyndi's List: cyndislist.com
British Library: bl.uk
National Archives Research Guides: nationalarchives.gov.uk/help-with-your-research/#find-a-research-guide
Wikipedia: en.wikipedia.org
National Archives Discovery Catalogue: discovery.nationalarchives.gov.uk
Eyewitness to History: eyewitnesstohistory.com
History Net: historynet.com

Timelines
BBC Timeline: bbc.co.uk/history/british/launch_tl_british.shtml
British Library Timeline: bl.uk/learning/histcitizen/timeline/accessvers
Victorian Web Timeline Industrial Revolution: victorianweb.org/technology/ir/irchron.html
BBC History Civil War and Revolution: www.bbc.co.uk/history/british/civil_war_revolution

Genealogy Websites and Databases
£ Ancestry: ancestry.co.uk
£ Findmypast: findmypast.co.uk
£ The Genealogist: thegenealogist.co.uk
Family History Centres: familysearch.org/locations/centerlocator

CHAPTER 2: PEOPLE, FAMILY AND SOCIETY
Demographics
Vision of Britain Through Time: bit.ly/VisionBritainPop
Michell, B.R. *British Historical Statistics*. (Cambridge: Cambridge University Press, 1988). Print.
Hist Pop: histpop.org

Case Study – Pig Street, Kingswinford
Old Maps Online: oldmapsonline.org
A Vision of Britain Through Time: visionofbritain.org.uk/place/8212
£ Ancestry: ancestry.co.uk
Hist Pop: histpop.org
British Library: bl.uk/collection-items/report-on-child-labour-1842

Ethnicity, Immigration and Social Currents
Punch Archive: punch.co.uk
Charles Booth Online Archive: booth.lse.ac.uk
Virtual Jewish World: jewishvirtuallibrary.org
£ Ancestry: ancestry.co.uk

Case Study – The Stockport Riots of June 1852
£ British Newspaper Archive: britishnewspaperarchive.co.uk
Trove Newspapers: trove.nla.gov.au/newspaper
Chronicling America: chroniclingamerica.loc.gov

Customs and Traditions
Samuel Pepys' Diary: pepysdiary.com

Case Study – Decorating the Church for Christmas
Cutts, Rev. Edward L. 'An Essay on the Christmas Decoration of
    Churches ... Illustrated. Reprinted, with Corrections and Additions,
    from the *Clerical Journal.*' Google Books. (1859). bit.ly/RevCutts.
Pattie, J., and G. Glaisher. *The Christmas Book: Christmas in the Olden
    Time, Its Customs and Their Origin : The Holly and Ivy, Sports of the
    Eve, Yule Log, Boar's Head, the Dinner, Mummers, Lord of Misrule,
    Saturnalia, Carols, Mysteries and Plays, Boxes, &c. &c.* Google Books.
    (1859). bit.ly/oldenchristmas.

Alcohol and Drugs
£ British Newspaper Archive: britishnewspaperarchive.co.uk
£ The Times Digital Archive: thetimes.co.uk/tto/archive (accessible
    free at many libraries)
Berridge, Virginia, and Griffith Edwards. *Opium and the People.* Drug
    Library. Web. bit.ly/OpiumPeople
Beeton, Isabella Mary. *The Book of Household Management.* Google
    Books. (1861). Web. bit.ly/Beeton
The Lancet - Issue 2 of 1858.' Google Books. (1858). bit.ly/lancet-
    addiction. 'Men and their Intoxicants', p. 41.

Case Study – Teetotallers
'Joseph Livesey: The Story of His Life, 1794-1884: Weston, James.'
    Internet Archive. 1884. bit.ly/JosephLivesey
£ British Newspaper Archive: britishnewspaperarchive.co.uk

Sexuality, Morality, Marriage and Divorce
Hist Pop: bit.ly/HistPopRegGen
£ Ancestry: bit.ly/AncestryDivorce
National Archives: nationalarchives.gov.uk/help-with-your-research/
  research-guides/divorces/
£ British Newspaper Archive: britishnewspaperarchive.co.uk

Case Study – Baby Farmers
£ British Newspaper Archive: britishnewspaperarchive.co.uk
The Old Bailey: oldbaileyonline.org

Children and Childhood
National Archives, Factory Act: nationalarchives.gov.uk/education/
  resources/1833-factory-act/
Parliament.uk, Education Act: parliament.uk/about/living-heritage/
  transformingsociety/livinglearning/school/overview/1870educationact/
The Old Bailey: oldbaileyonline.org

Case Study – Child Labour Reform
British Newspaper Archive: britishnewspaperarchive.co.uk
Ancestry: ancestry.co.uk
Grant, Philip, and Anthony Ashley Cooper. 'The Ten Hours Bill.'
  Google Books. (1866). bit.ly/TenHoursBill.

CHAPTER 3: DOMESTIC AFFAIRS
Environment
Richards, Henry Charles, and William Henry Christoper Payne. *The
  Metropolitan Water Supply*. Google Books. (1891).
  bit.ly/LondonWater.

Case Study – Public Health
Hime, Thomas Whiteside. 'Public Health; the Practical Guide to the
  Public Health Act, 1875, and Correlated Acts: Thomas Whiteside
  Hime : Internet Archive.' Internet Archive. 1884.
  bit.ly/PubHealth1875.
£ British Newspaper Archive: britishnewspaperarchive.co.uk

Clothing and Fashion

The Gentleman's Magazine of Fashion. Google Books. (1870).
  bit.ly/GentMag.

Thomas, Mrs Edward. *The London and Paris Ladies' Magazine of
  Fashion, Ed. by Mrs Edward Thomas.* Google Books. (1885).
  bit.ly/LadiesLondonParis.

Fashion-Era: fashion-era.com

Victoria & Albert Museum: vam.ac.uk

Books by Maureen Taylor: bit.ly/WikiMaureenTaylor

Case Study – The Trench Coat

Espacenet Patent Search: epo.org

Burberry: uk.burberry.com

Aquascutum: aquascutum.com

£ British Newspaper Archive: britishnewspaperarchive.co.uk

Food and Cooking

Bishop, Frederick. *The Illustrated London Cookery Book.* Google Books.
  (1852). bit.ly/CookBook1852.

Cobbett, Anne. *The English Housekeeper: Or, Manual of Domestic
  Management, Etc.* Google Books. (1835). bit.ly/EngHouseKeeper.

Ridgway, James. *British Farmer's Magazine.* Google Books. (1839).
  bit.ly/FarmersMag.

Case Study – Stealing to Eat

£ British Newspaper Archive: britishnewspaperarchive.co.uk

The Old Bailey: oldbaileyonline.org

Workhouses: workhouses.org.uk

House and Home

The Geffry Museum of the Home: geffrye-museum.org.uk

Historic England: historicengland.org.uk/listing/the-list/

Case Study – The Flood

Sheffield Flood Archives: www2.shu.ac.uk/sfca/

Harrison, S. *A Complete History of the Great Flood at Sheffield on March
  11 & 12, 1864.* Google Books. (1864). bit.ly/SheffieldFlood.

£ British Newspaper Archive: britishnewspaperarchive.co.uk

£ Ancestry: ancestry.co.uk

Housekeeping
Scott, William. *The House Book ; Or, Family Chronicle of Useful Knowledge, and Cottage Physician.* Google Books. (1826). bit.ly/HouseBook.
Old and Interesting: oldandinteresting.com

Case Study – The Housekeeper
Beeton, Isabella Mary. *The Book of Household Management.* Google Books. (1861). Web. bit.ly/Beeton

Land and Property
National Archives (Land Records Guide): nationalarchives.gov.uk/help-with-your-research/research-guides/enrolment-of-deeds-registration-of-titles-land/
National Archives (Probate 1384-1858): nationalarchives.gov.uk/help-with-your-research/research-guides/wills-1384-1858
£ Ancestry (Probate after 1858): ancestry.co.uk
£ The Genealogist Tithe Maps: thegenealogist.co.uk/featuredarticles/2015/the-tithe-maps-project-317
£ The Genealogist Land Owner Records: thegenealogist.co.uk
Fire Insurance Maps: bl.uk/onlinegallery/onlineex/firemaps/fireinsurancemaps.html

Case Study– Streetlam Castle Farm
£ The Genealogist: thegenealogist.co.uk

CHAPTER 4: BIRTH, LIFE AND DEATH
Birth
GRO (General Register Office, Certificates): gro.gov.uk/gro/content/certificates/
Family Search: familysearch.org
£ Ancestry: ancestry.co.uk
£ Findmypast: findmypast.co.uk
£ The Genealogist: thegenealogist.co.uk
jStor: jstor.org
Google Books: books.google.co.uk
Internet Archives: archive.org

Case Study – Manslaughter in Childbirth Death
£ British Newspaper Archive: britishnewspaperarchive.co.uk
£ Ancestry (England & Wales, Criminal Registers, 1791-1892): ancestry.co.uk

Health and Lifestyle
About.com Family Health History: genealogy.about.com/library/ authors/ucbishop7a.htm
Geneweaver (family health history tool): geneweaveronline.com

Case Study – The Bicycling Craze of the 1890s
£ British Newspaper Archive: britishnewspaperarchive.co.uk
Cycling UK (History): cyclinguk.org/history

Medicine
Palluault, Florent. *Medical students in England and France, 1815-1858: a comparative study*. (2004). Print.
National Archives, Hospital Records Database: nationalarchives. gov.uk/hospitalrecords/

Case Study – The London Smallpox Hospital
£ British Newspaper Archive (*Ipswich Journal* 1758): britishnewspaper archive.co.uk

Diseases and Epidemics
£ British Newspaper Archive: britishnewspaperarchive.co.uk
jStor: jstor.org
Google Books: books.google.co.uk
Internet Archives: archive.org
Wellcome Library: wellcomelibrary.org

Case Study – Scarlet Fever and the Economy
Scott, Susan, and Christopher J. Duncan. *Human Demography and Disease*. Google Books. (1998). bit.ly/24dfoJB.
£ British Newspaper Archive: britishnewspaperarchive.co.uk

Mental Health
Bethlem Museum of the Mind: museumofthemind.org.uk

Andrew Robert's Home Page: studymore.org.uk

National Archives (Mental Health): nationalarchives.gov.uk/help-with-your-research/research-guides/mental-health/

National Archives, Hospital Records Database: nationalarchives.gov.uk/hospitalrecords/

£ Ancestry: ancestry.co.uk

£ Findmypast: findmypast.co.uk

Case Study – The York Retreat

The York Retreat, History: theretreatyork.org.uk/history/

£ British Newspaper Archive: britishnewspaperarchive.co.uk

£ Ancestry: ancestry.co.uk

Thurnam, John. *Observations and Essays on the Statistics of Insanity.* Google Books. (1845). bit.ly/EssaysInsanity.

Mortality

Office for National Statistics. 'Article: Mortality in England and Wales: Average Life Span, 2010.' Mortality in England and Wales – Office for National Statistics. 2012. bit.ly/1WHUqBi.

Hist Pop: histpop.org

Office for National Statistics (ONS): bit.ly/ONSLifeExp

£ British Newspaper Archive: britishnewspaperarchive.co.uk

Case Study – Centenarian

£ British Newspaper Archive: britishnewspaperarchive.co.uk

£ Ancestry: ancestry.co.uk

Death and Burials

Find-a-Grave: findagrave.com

Hartley, Florence. *The Ladies' Book of Etiquette, and Manual of Politeness.* Google Books. (1872). bit.ly/MourningEtiquette. P. 82.

Tegg, W. *The Last Act: Being the Funeral Rites of Nations and Individuals.* Google Books. (1876). bit.ly/TheLastAct.

Case Study – Baron Heath's Funeral

£ British Newspaper Archive: britishnewspaperarchive.co.uk

£ Ancestry: ancestry.co.uk

CHAPTER 5: WORK, WAGES AND ECONOMY

Economy

Measuring Worth: www.measuringworth.com

The Victorian Web (Economics): victorianweb.org/economics/index.html

The East India Company Timeline: theeastindiacompany.com/index.php/24/timeline

Bank of England (History): www.bankofengland.co.uk/about/Pages/history/default.aspx

Case Study – Riot in Barrow-Upon-Soar 1795

£ British Newspaper Archives: britishnewspaperarchives.co.uk

Occupations

Vision of Britain Through Time: visionofbritain.org.uk

Family Search Wiki, England Occupations: familysearch.org/learn/wiki/en/England_Occupations

Historical Directories of England and Wales, University of Leicester: specialcollections.le.ac.uk/cdm/landingpage/collection/ p16445coll4

Welton, Thomas Abercrombie. *Statistical Papers Based on the Census of England and Wales, 1851: And Relating to the Occupations of the People and the Increase of Population, 1841-51*. Google Books. (London: Printed for the Author by Savill and Edwards, 1860). bit.ly/CensusOcc

Abercrombie, John, and Thomas Mawe. *Every Man His Own Gardener: Being a New, and Much More Complete Gardener's Kalendar, and General Director, Than Any One Hitherto Published*. Google Books. (London: Printed for J.F. and C. Rivington, T. Longman, B. Law, J. Johnson, G.G.J. and J. Robinson [and 6 others in London], 1787). bit.ly/HistGarden.

Bradley, Tom. *Old Coaching Days in Yorkshire*. Google Books. (Leeds: Yorkshire Conservative Newspaper Co, 1889). bit.ly/CoachingDays

Stott, John. 'On the Mortality among Innkeepers, Publicans, and other Persons engaged in the Sale of Intoxicating Liquors, — being the Experience of the Scottish Amicable Life Assurance Society during Fifty Years, 1826-1876'. jStor. *Journal of the Institute of Actuaries and Assurance Magazine* Vol. 20, No. 1 (October 1876), pp. 35–43.

Case Study – Framework Knitters

£ British Newspaper Archive: britishnewspaperarchive.co.uk

£ Ancestry: ancestry.co.uk

Framework Knitters Museum: frameworkknittersmuseum.org.uk

Businesses and Employers

Historical Directories of England and Wales, University of Leicester: specialcollections.le.ac.uk/cdm/landingpage/collection/ p16445coll4

Google Books: books.google.co.uk

Internet Archive: archive.org

£ British Newspaper Archive: britishnewspaperarchive.co.uk

National Archives Discovery: discovery.nationalarchives.gov.uk

Thomas Cook Archives: thomascook.com/thomas-cook-archives

Case Study – Barrow Ship Building Company

Grace's Guide to British Industrial History: www.gracesguide.co.uk

Early Factory Legislation: parliament.uk/about/living-heritage/ transformingsociety/livinglearning/19thcentury/overview/earlyfactor ylegislation

The 1833 Factory Act: parliament.uk/about/living-heritage/ transformingsociety/livinglearning/19thcentury/overview/factoryact

Later Factory Legislation: parliament.uk/about/living-heritage/ transformingsociety/livinglearning/19thcentury/overview/laterfactor yleg

Social Welfare and Relief

The Victorian Web: 'The Price of Bread: Poverty, Purchasing Power, and The Victorian Laborer's Standard of Living' by Robert L. Nelson, MD: victorianweb.org/history/work/nelson1.html

Evans, Sir William David. *A Collection of Statutes Connected with the General Administration, Volume 8.* Google Books. (London: Thomas Blenkarn, Edward Lumley and W.H. Bond, 1836). bit.ly/StatutesUK

Poor Law Commissioners. *Annual Report of the Poor Law Commissioners for England and Wales, Volume 2.* Google Books. (London: W. Clowes and Sons, 1836).

Aschrott, Paul Felix. *The English Poor Law System, Past and Present.* Google Books. (London: Knight & Co., 1888). bit.ly/PoorLawUK

Workhouses: workhouses.org.uk

Higginbotham, Peter. *The Workhouse Encylopedia*. (Stroud, Gloucestershire: History Press, 2012).

Higginbotham, Peter. *Life in A Victorian Workhouse*. (Stroud, Gloucestershire: History Press, 2011).

London Lives: londonlives.org.uk

Charles Booth Online Archive: booth.lse.ac.uk

Case Study – The Cycle of Poverty

Charles Booth Online Archive: booth.lse.ac.uk

£ Ancestry (Parish, census, workhouse): ancestry.co.uk

CHAPTER 6 – COMMUNITY, RELIGION AND GOVERNMENT
Community

'The Foresters Heritage Trust – The History of the Foresters Friendly Society.' The Foresters Heritage Trust – The History of the Foresters Friendly Society. aoforestersheritage.com/Research_enquiries.html.

'Home – The Library and Museum of Freemasonry.' The Library and Museum of Freemasonry. freemasonry.london.museum.

Lane's Masonic Records, version 1.0 (hrionline.ac.uk/lane, October 2011). Published by HRI Online Publications, ISBN 978-0-955-7876-8-3.

'Welcome to the Oddfellows Friendly Society Website.' The Oddfellows. oddfellows.co.uk/OnlineArchives.

Case Study – The Spinning School

An Account of Two Charity Schools for the Education of Girls: And of a Female Friendly Society in York: Interspersed with Reflections on Charity Schools and Friendly Societies in General. Google Books. (1800). bit.ly/CharitySchools.

Markets and Fairs

The Gazetteer of Markets and Fairs in England and Wales to 1516: history.ac.uk/cmh/gaz/gazweb2.html

Owen, William. *Owen's New Book of Fairs: Published by the King's Authority*: William Owen: Internet Archive. archive.org/details/owensnewbookfai00owengoog.

£ British Newspaper Archive: britishnewspaperarchive.co.uk

Goose Fair of Nottinghamshire: nottinghamcity.gov.uk/events-markets-parks-and-museums/events-in-nottingham

Case Study – Northallerton Markets

Owen, William. *Owen's New Book of Fairs: Published by the King's Authority*: William Owen: Internet Archive. archive.org/details/owensnewbookfai00owengoog.

£ British Newspaper Archive: britishnewspaperarchive.co.uk

Education, Language and Literacy

Mitch, David. 'Education and Skill of the British Labour Force', in Floud, Roderick, and Paul Johnson (eds), *The Cambridge Economic History of Modern Britain, Vol. I: Industrialisation, 1700-1860.* (Cambridge: Cambridge University Press, 2004), p. 344.

Watson, William Henry. 'The History of the Sunday School Union: William Henry Watson: Internet Archive.' Internet Archive. 1853. archive.org/details/historysundaysc00watsgoog.

£ Ancestry: ancestry.co.uk

£ Findmypast: findmypast.co.uk

School Records: schoolrecords.org.uk

£ British Newspaper Archive: britishnewspaperarchive.co.uk

Case Study – Burslem School Attendance Officer

£ British Newspaper Archive: britishnewspaperarchive.co.uk

£ Ancestry: ancestry.co.uk

Religion and Church

Parliament UK (search law of marriage): parliament.uk

Legislation UK (search burial act): legislation.gov.uk

National Archives (1851 Ecclesiastical Census returns from Sheffield): bit.ly/1851Sheffield

The 'Million Act' Churches of Yorkshire: genuki.org.uk/big/eng/ YKS/Misc/CBW/YPRsMillionAct.html

£ British Newspaper Archive: britishnewspaperarchive.co.uk

Case Study – St Philips Church, Sheffield

Great Britain Census Office, and Horace Mann, Esq. *Census of Great Britain, 1851: Religious Worship in England and Wales*: Great Britain Census Office, Horace Mann: Internet Archive. 1854. bit.ly/EccCensus1851.

Sheffield FHS (Parish Churches): sheffieldfhs.org.uk/services-data/
   sheffield-parish-churches/
National Archives (1851 Ecclesiastical Census returns from Sheffield):
   bit.ly/1851Sheffield
£ British Newspaper Archive: britishnewspaperarchive.co.uk

Persecution
Huguenot Society of London: huguenotsociety.org.uk
Catholic Family History Society: catholicfhs.co.uk
National Archives Jewish Research: bit.ly/TNAJewishResearch
London Metropolitan Archives – Jewish Life: bit.ly/LondonMetJewish
   Archives
Google Books: books.google.co.uk
Internet Archive: archive.org
£ British Newspaper Archive: britishnewspaperarchive.co.uk

Case Study – The Gordon Riots
£ British Newspaper Archive: britishnewspaperarchive.co.uk
National Archives – The Gordon Riots: nationalarchives.gov.uk/
   pathways/blackhistory/rights/gordon.htm
The Victorian Web – The Gordon Riots: victorianweb.org/history/
   riots/gordon.html
British Library – The Gordon Riots: bl.uk/learning/timeline/
   item104674.html

Crime and Punishment
Old Bailey: oldbaileyonline.org
£ British Newspaper Archive: britishnewspaperarchive.co.uk
Google Books: books.google.co.uk
Internet Archive: archive.org
£ Ancestry: ancestry.co.uk
£ Findmypast: findmypast.co.uk
Convict Records: convictrecords.com.au
York Family History Society – York Assizes: yorkfamilyhistory.org.uk/
   resources/york-assizes/
Fortescue, Lincoln. *The Life and Adventures of Jack Sheppard*. Google
   Books. (1845). bit.ly/JackSheppard.

Case Study – Pleading their Bellies
Old Bailey: oldbaileyonline.org
£ Ancestry: ancestry.co.uk
£ British Newspaper Archive: britishnewspaperarchive.co.uk

War, Revolution and Unrest
Anglo Boer War: angloboerwar.com
Families in British India Society – fibis.org
First World War: firstworldwar.com
Windham, Sir Charles Ash, Hugh Wodehouse Pearse, and Sir William Howard Russell. *The Crimean Diary and Letters of Lieut.-General Sir Charles Ash Windham*: Windham, Charles Ash, Sir, 1810-1870 : Internet Archive. 1897. bit.ly/CrimeanDiary.

Case Study – Wounded at Braklaagte
£ British Newspaper Archive: britishnewspaperarchive.co.uk
Anglo Boer War: angloboerwar.com
South African History Online: sahistory.org.za/article/first-anglo-boer-war

INDEX

Church Building Commission, 166–7
Church of England, 50–1, 56, 150, 164–5, 169
cities, industrial (also urban), 36, 66, 100, 109
city cemeteries, 122
city directories, 19, 102, 139
civil marriages, 51, 165
civil registration certificates, 136
classes, 47, 94, 105, 143
    lower, 23–4, 57, 77
    upper, 23, 51–2, 57, 76, 102
clubs, 101–2, 148–9, 152, 154–6
    burial, 120
coal, 26, 38, 65, 77, 81, 84, 132
coal miners, 26–8, 57
colonies, 4, 59, 124, 151, 170
    penal, 59
commercial directories, 109
commissions, 62, 68, 104, 133, 143
companies. *See* businesses
Companies' Registration Office records, 140
conditions
    living, 63
    unsanitary, 66, 109, 117
    working, 100
conflicts, 150–1, 169, 177
Congregationalists, 150
Convict Records, 176
cookbooks, 76
corn, 45, 76, 158
Corn Laws, 110–11
coroner, 46, 139
Coroner's inquest, 177
corsets, 63, 69–70

cottage industries, 130, 132, 136, 156
cotton, 65, 124
County Lunatic Asylums, 116
county record offices, 99, 116, 147
court records, 53, 68, 75
crimes, 18, 59, 147, 169, 172–7
    criminal records, 56, 176
customs and traditions, 2–3, 22, 36, 38, 40, 42–3, 121, 123
cycling. *See* bicycle
Cyndi's List, 17, 147

D
data
    demographical, 25, 30
    statistical, 24, 55
death, 13, 20, 23, 25, 30, 44, 46, 52, 65–6, 92–6, 100, 103, 109–10, 116, 119–23
    cause of, 46, 103–4, 109
death records, 48, 103, 107, 121–2, 134
debts, 38, 151
decimalization, 126
deeds, 91, 134
demographics, 2, 14, 19, 24–5
depression
    clinical, 112, 114
    economic, 110
dialects, 10, 149
diaries and letters, 4, 7, 14–15, 18, 38, 43, 140, 180
diets, 72, 74, 76, 92, 99–100, 107
digitized books, 5–9, 20, 29, 62, 71, 76, 80, 123, 134, 172, 180
digitized directories, 139